OLDHAM CORPORATION TRAMWAYS

By
ARTHUR KIRBY B.Sc., B.A.(Com.)

To my late wife, Elspeth

CONTENTS

Plate 1. The formal opening of the Oldham tramways on Whit Monday 19th May 1902, showing the eight decorated cars lined up outside the Town Hall. This marked the opening of the main route from Hollinwood to Waterhead but the first electric services had commenced on 15th December 1900 on Middleton Road.

Photo, F & G Pollard

Plate 2. A scene about 1903 showing an open top tram in High Street.

Photo, Valentine's Series

Plate 3. This view, probably taken on the same day as that of the previous one, shows a scene in Yorkshire Street, the continuation of High Street.

Photo, Valentine's Series

AUTHOR'S NOTE

AS a boy I lived on Manchester's 53 tram route which, alone of the city's extensive tramway network, was operated by single-deck vehicles because of low railway bridges. This was Manchester's busiest route, accounting for about 8% of the passengers carried on the system, and on account of the irregular service resulting from extensive sections of single-track, it was the first of the city's tramways to be converted to bus operation, in March 1930. Over 30 years later I became aware of a plan to restore the body of one of these trams which had been recovered from a farm at Slaithwaite in West Yorkshire. To help finance this project I wrote a history of the 53 route which was published in November 1964, marking the 60th Anniversary of its opening. In compiling this history I found that Manchester had acquired 10 trams, from the Middleton Electric Traction Company, some of which had been used on the 53 route.

When time permitted I researched the history of this Company and of the tramways generally in Middleton, the outcome of which was the publication of Middleton Tramways in October 1976. The section of the Company's line in Chadderton was acquired in 1925 by Oldham whose trams I had seen in Manchester at the end of the War as they turned from Lever Street briefly into Piccadilly before returning to Oldham by Oldham Street. My interest having been aroused, the opportunity to pursue this subject in detail had to wait until my retirement from business life in October 1988.

This volume relies very heavily on many visits to the Local Studies Centre of Oldham Library in Union Street, and I am particularly indebted to Mrs. Terry Berry, Local History Officer and her staff, whose detailed records of files and documents led to a gratifying amount of fascinating detail and facts about the Oldham Tramways.

I must also thank Roy Brook of Huddersfield for extracting relevant items on Oldham on his periodic visits to the Public Record Office at Kew. Eric Fielding has provided useful detail and photographs. Other specific points have been resolved by consulting material at the Manchester Central Library in the Commercial, Local History and Archives Departments, to whose staff I am indebted. Statistical information was provided by Birmingham Central Library Social Sciences Department, Lancashire County Public Record Office, Preston, and the Greater Manchester Transport Museum. Cyril Kidd readily made available a selection of tickets.

The information on withdrawal dates of trams in the earlier years relies heavily on the work of Mr. G. G. Hilditch, and for vehicle types, the records of Mr. George Lawton, made available by Chris Heaps.

A history of this nature relies very heavily for its interest on its photographic content, and I am indebted to the photographers and publishers whose work is included; they are acknowledged where known, but regrettably in some cases original sources are not known. The work of Messrs W. A. Camwell, M. J. O'Connor, and H. B. Priestley is included courtesy of The National Tramway Museum.

The length of this narrative extended steadily over the years as information came to light and I am most grateful to Miss Pam Harrison for continually updating the information by word processor. Mr. Alan Palmer has kindly produced the excellent maps.

I have refrained from quoting distances in metric terms but in order to avoid the use of furlongs and chains have used only miles and yards, noting that there are 1,760 yards in one mile. The severe inflation in the post war years renders items quoted in pounds sterling rather meaningless so in the more appropriate cases and in order to give readers the feel of prices generally over the tramway period, I have quoted the present day equivalent in brackets. These conversions are based on data issued by the Bank of England.

Arthur Kirby, Bramhall,1998

Plate 4. Further along Yorkshire Street a passing loop gave way to a short section of interlaced track seen here in this early view which shows clearly the ornamental ironwork on the tram standards. *Photo, Abel Heywood & Son*

Plate 5. The photographer is looking ahead to Union Street West, with King Street crossing in the foreground.
Photo, F & G Pollard

INTRODUCTION

OLDHAM is one of several towns on the periphery of Manchester, lying 6½ miles to the North East. It was incorporated as a borough in June 1849 and became a county borough in 1888. It lies on the western slopes of the Pennine hills, rising from an altitude of some 400 feet above sea level on its southern fringes to 700 feet in the town centre, and to 1,000 feet at Grains Bar at its northern boundary.

The town saw rapid growth in the 19th century under the stimulus of the industrial revolution and a developing transport network. The Lancashire and Yorkshire Railway opened its line from Manchester to Littleborough on 4th July 1839 and a branch line at Middleton Junction to Werneth followed on 31st March 1842. This was extended within the town to Mumps on 1st November 1847. The Lancashire and North Western Railway opened a route from Stalybridge to Huddersfield, passing east of Oldham, on 1st August 1849 and connected this from Greenfield to Oldham via Lees on 5th July 1856. Further connection to Oldham was provided on 26th August 1861 when the Oldham, Ashton & Guide Bridge Junction railway provided a route from the south to Clegg Street. The Lancashire and Yorkshire Railway extended its tracks on 12th August 1863 northerly through Shaw and Crompton to Rochdale and provided a branch from this to Royton on 21st March in the following year. Lastly, the same Company provided a more direct route from Manchester by the opening on 17th May 1880 of its line through Failsworth and Hollinwood, parallelling the main road from Manchester, and meeting its original line at Werneth. The lines from Oldham thus radiated north, south, east and west. Through closures in the 1960s only the line from Manchester via Hollinwood to Rochdale now remains. The contours of the district generally precluded canals, but Hollinwood, a low lying district, was served by a branch of the Manchester and Ashton-under-Lyne canal.

Horse tramways were introduced in November 1880 running through Oldham from Hollinwood to Waterhead, and in August 1885 steam trams commenced to run through the Borough from Royton to the boundary at Hathershaw.

Oldham became the centre of the fine cotton spinning industry which in keeping with the cotton textile industry generally expanded strongly until 1913. Since then output and employment declined almost continuously as export markets were lost and the home market became increasingly supplied by newer overseas competitors. The district also developed strongly in engineering, much of it related to the needs of the cotton industry and here again the pattern reflected that of the cotton industry on which it was based.

At the present time, Oldham has a more diverse economy with many manufacturers housed in former spinning mills. Textile activities now comprise mainly specialised high value-added items such as those produced by Seton Healthcare, and in engineering by companies such as Coin Controls which manufactures coin handling equipment and mechanisms for world markets. The population expanded from 137,246 in 1901 to 144,983 in 1921 but declined to 140,314 in 1931 and to 121,266 in 1951. Population in the area served by the tramways was 203,955 in 1931.

Under local government reorganisation which came into effect on 1st April 1974, Oldham absorbed the adjoining urban districts of Failsworth, Chadderton, Royton, Crompton, Lees and Saddleworth. Part of the rural district of Limehurst had been absorbed by Oldham on 1st April 1951. The general pattern of employment in this enlarged area over the years has not been dissimilar from that of Oldham itself, the former dependence on cotton textiles having declined as the industry shrank.

This history of Oldham Corporation Tramways necessarily extends beyond the former county borough's boundaries since it provided the tramway services at varying times in Chadderton, Royton, Crompton and Lees; the Failsworth tramways were leased to Manchester, although as will be seen later, Oldham trams operated over them.

EARLY TRAMWAYS

IT is not the purpose of this history to cover in any detail the horse and steam tramways which provided local transport before they were superseded by Oldham's introduction of electric tramways. Nevertheless, a brief reference is necessary in order to set the scene for municipal operation.

The key legislation governing the operation of tramways was the Tramways Act 1870 under which promoters could apply for Tramway Orders or promote local Tramway Acts. Local authorities were enabled to own tracks but were required to lease them unless this was impossible at an economic rent.

In the Manchester area a horse tram service between Pendleton and Kersal commenced on 18th May 1877, and from this grew an extensive network ranging from Eccles in the West to Stalybridge in the East, to Oldham in the North East and to Stockport in the South East, all operated by the Manchester Carriage and Tramways Company. Some of the tracks were owned by the company and others, generally in the larger municipalities, by the local authority, and this applied in the case of Oldham.

The original lines in Oldham were authorised by the Oldham Borough Tramways Order, 1878, confirmed by the Tramways Orders Confirmation Act, 1878 (No. 2) which conferred powers for the construction of the following tramways:

1. A single line four miles 112 yards long commencing at the boundary with Failsworth in Manchester Road, continuing along Manchester Street, Market Place, High Street, Yorkshire Street, Mumps, Bottom o'th' Moor and Huddersfield Road to the boundary with Springhead near Culvert Street.

2. A single line 1,412 yards long forming a double track with tramway No. 1 from its commencement to a junction with it in Manchester Road near Old Lane.

3-9. These were seven passing places at various points along the route of tramway No. 1, each 44 yards long, apart from tramway No. 4 which was 132 yards long located in Manchester Road between Edward Street and Porter Street.

10. A single line 1 mile 134 yards long in Huddersfield Road forming a double track with tramway No. 1 from junctions with it at Shaw Road and Church Street East.

11. A single line 1,462 yards long commencing by a junction with tramway No. 1 at Crossbank Street, passing along Crossbank Street, Union Street West, Union Street and Yorkshire Street terminating by a junction with tramway No. 1 18 yards west of Coronation Street.

12. A single line 975 yards long wholly in Union Street forming a double track with tramway No. 11 from junctions with it at King Street and Coronation Street.

Horse trams commenced to operate over these lines on 1st November 1880, connecting at Hollinwood when services from Manchester opened on 28th March 1881; the gauge was 4ft. 8½ins.

The Manchester, Bury, Rochdale and Oldham Steam Tramways Company Limited was formed to operate steam tramways in the areas indicated by the title. The promoters obtained powers to construct tramways in Bury and Rochdale, but Oldham insisted that any lines in Oldham must be built by the borough and leased to the company. Powers were duly obtained under the Oldham Improvement Act, 1880, for operation of tramways in the borough by "steam power or any mechanical power", whilst The Oldham Borough Tramways (Extensions) Order, 1882 confirmed by the Tramways Orders Confirmation (No. 1) Act, 1882, authorised the construction of further lines as follows:-

1. A line 2 miles 639 yards long comprising 1 mile 1,475 yards single and 924 yards of double track commencing in Rochdale Road at the boundary with Royton (Boundary Street), along Rochdale Road, Saint Domingo Street, King Street and Ashton Road terminating in Ashton Road at the boundary with Limehurst rural district (Fir Tree Avenue). The 924 yards of double track comprised 14 passing loops each of 66 yards.

2. A curve 26 yards long connecting tramway No. 1 at a point in King Street north of the junction with Union Street West with tramway No. 11 authorised by the 1878 Order at a point in Union Street east of King Street.

3. A curve 38 yards long connecting tramway No. 1 at a point in King Street south of the junction with Union Street West with tramway No. 11 authorised by the 1878 Order at a point in Union Street east of King Street.

4. A line 1 mile 376 yards long comprising 1,730 yards single and 406 yards of double track commencing in Rochdale Road by a junction with tramway No. 1, along Featherstall Road North and

Featherstall Road South terminating in Manchester Road by a junction with tramway No. 4 authorised by the 1878 Order. The double track comprised six passing loops, five each of 66 yards, and one of 76 yards.

5. A single line 45 yards long in Manchester Road forming, with tramway No. 4, a double track section to its terminal point.

A service of steam trams from Dogford Road, Royton, along Rochdale Road and through Oldham to the boundary at Fir Tree Avenue on Ashton Road, commenced on 1st August 1885; the tracks were again laid to standard gauge i.e. 4ft. 8½in., a condition imposed by Oldham given that the horse trams were operating to this gauge. North of Dogford Road, where the depot was situated, the gauge was 3ft. 6in.

It was mentioned earlier that local authorities were not allowed to operate tramways but this situation changed in the 1895–1896 Session of Parliament when the House of Commons Standing Order which imposed this prohibition was revoked. Naturally, many local authorities began to investigate the possibility of operating tramways themselves. Manchester, for example, obtained powers to operate, and to use electric traction, under the Manchester Corporation Act 1897, and on 1st December, the City Council decided to take over operation of the horse tramways at the expiration of the existing leases.

The Oldham Town Clerk had been monitoring developments in Manchester, and as early as May 1897 had drawn attention to the fact that both Manchester and Salford were promoting Bills giving powers to operate tramways, and thought Oldham should do the same before the existing leases expired in 1901. Again, in August, he alerted Oldham to the fact that Manchester was seeking powers to acquire the Manchester Carriage and Tramways Company and thought Oldham should deal similarly with the two companies in its area; however, the situation was somewhat different in that neither company owned any assets in Oldham and operation could cease simply by Oldham not renewing the leases.

Given that the Carriage Company was operating in the areas of many local authorities, Manchester invited representatives from these to a conference on 19th January 1898, to consider future arrangements. It was agreed that Manchester would operate in its own area and also provide the services in ten surrounding urban districts, including Failsworth, which lay between Manchester and Oldham. Oldham decided to work its own system, as did Salford, Ashton, Stockport, and, in a consortium, Stalybridge.

Plate 6. The side poles with bracket arms supporting the overhead had even more elaborate scroll work than the conventional side pole, as is shown by this view in Egerton Street. After interrupted service Egerton Street finally lost its tram service before the first World War, and some of the equipment was used on the Grains Bar extension.

MIDDLETON DEVELOPMENTS

IT is now necessary to have a look at developments in nearby Middleton because of their bearing on the Oldham scene. The British Electric Traction Company (BET) was actively promoting tramway schemes throughout the British Isles and in October 1897 informed Oldham that a draft Order under The Light Railways Act 1896 would shortly be issued to authorise the construction of lines centred on Middleton, extending into Castleton and Chadderton Urban Districts, and Oldham. BET explained that powers were being sought under The Light Railways Act rather than The Tramways Act because the former provided an opportunity for discussion of the proposals at a local Enquiry held by The Light Railway Commissioners. The proposals were considered by the Commissioners at an Enquiry held in Middleton on 5th February 1898. Middleton was generally in favour of the proposals but unhappy that the application had been made under the Light Railways Act rather than the Tramways Act, since it considered the former appropriate for rural districts rather than urban areas such as Middleton.

The basic objection related to the powers for acquisition by Middleton: under the Tramways Act a local authority could purchase after 21 years, in effect at asset value and without any allowance for goodwill. Under the Light Railways Act an Order could contain provisions empowering purchase by the local authority and in this instance BET was seeking a clause allowing purchase after 35 years and subsequently at 10 year intervals, at the fair market value as a going concern. Middleton pressed for a clause allowing purchase after 21 years at capital value less depreciation, together with a sum representing any deficiency relative to an annual 5% dividend over the whole period. Eventually, on 8th June, the Commissioners agreed to grant the Order, including powers for the local authorities to purchase the undertaking, but at the end of 25 years on a going concern basis without any allowance for compulsory purchase.

The Order then had to be confirmed by the Board of Trade, who heard Middleton's objections on 19th October. Middleton reiterated that 25 years was an excessive period before it could exercise purchase powers and that in any case the basis of purchase should be the value of the property at date of purchase after due allowance for depreciation, and not as a going concern. Oldham, which had previously insisted that the Commissioners had no powers to hear the case relating to the Oldham section (350 yards), objected to the proposal given that it was then applying for powers to operate tramways and construct additional lines (duly confirmed in its 1899 Act). Despite Middleton's objections the Board of Trade confirmed the Order on 15th December 1898, creating something of a precedent given that the local authority had objected.

The Middleton Light Railways Order, 1898, authorised the construction of 8 miles 1,397 yards of light railways extending from Middleton to Prestwich, Castleton and, through Chadderton, to Oldham. The last mentioned line (railway 2b) was 3 miles 37 yards long comprising 2 miles 633 yards of single and 1,164 yards of double track from Market Place Middleton along Townley Street, Oldham Road, Middleton Road West and Middleton Road terminating in Middleton Road five yards west of Featherstall Road North and Featherstall Road South. Railways 2c and 2d were curves 22 yards long connecting railway 2b with the Oldham Corporation tracks in Featherstall Road South and Featherstall Road North respectively.

Oldham's objections were accepted by the Board of Trade to the extent that under the terms of the Order, the company was not allowed to construct the lines in Oldham without Oldham's consent until two years had elapsed from the commencement of the Order; if within that time Oldham constructed and opened tramways between its boundary with Chadderton and Featherstall Road North, then the powers lapsed. The company was, however, allowed to agree running powers with the Bury, Rochdale & Oldham Tramways Company Limited (the successor to the Manchester, Bury, Rochdale and Oldham Steam Tramway), with the consent of Oldham, over any part of the steam company's tramway system. As noted later, Oldham obtained powers (tramway No. 3) under its 1899 Act which received the Royal Assent on 9th August, to construct the line from the Chadderton boundary to Oldham. During consideration of the Bill BET vainly sought Middleton's support for the company's petition for running powers in Oldham, which was unsuccessful. The Middleton company's Order commenced on 15th December 1898 so that the time limit allowed to Oldham to construct the line to Chadderton expired on 15th December 1900.

Plate 7. Car No. 30 stands at the terminus in Hollins Road in the early days of the system. The tracks in the foreground are in Manchester Road leading to the Hollinwood terminus on the right. Behind the nearer horse drawn cart can be seen a time-keeping clock.

Plate 8. Further along Hollins Road a tram is seen entering one of the passing loops on its journey to Hollinwood.

Plate 9. A view taken about 1905 at the intersection with King Street showing Union Street with its centre poles. These were removed in 1920 because of the increasing possibility of accidents arising from the growing volume of road traffic; the wires were then mainly suspended from rosettes attached to the buildings.

Photo, Abel Heywood & Son

OLDHAM CORPORATION ACT, 1899

IT seems fairly clear that BET's action stimulated Oldham's thinking. At a special meeting of the Surveyor's Committee, held on 27th July 1898, it was decided to recommend the Council to promote a Bill to operate and extend the tramways with the hope that other local authorities in the Parliamentary Constituencey of Oldham would do the same. Reflecting the new emphasis the Committee was renamed the Surveyors and Tramways Committee on 6th March 1899. As early as April, a tender from Barrow Haematite Steel Company for the supply of tramway rails was accepted subject to Oldham's Bill becoming law. This duly came to pass as the Oldham Corporation Act 1899. The lines authorised were:

1. A line 1,593 yards long comprising 1,054 yards single and 539 yards of double track commencing in Chadderton Road at the boundary with Chadderton (Westhulme Avenue), along Chadderton Road, Barker Street and Henshaw Street terminating in Market Place by a junction with the existing tramway (No. 1 of the 1878 Order).

1a. A single line 39 yards long connecting No. 1 in Henshaw Street with the existing tramway in Market Place.

2. A line 1,122 yards long comprising 792 yards single and 330 yards of double track commencing in Albion Street, along Albion Street, Rock Street, Radcliffe Street and Egerton Street terminating in Shaw Road by a junction with tramway No. 7.

3. A line 1,121 yards long comprising 857 yards single and 264 yards of double track commencing in Middleton Road at the boundary with Chadderton (just beyond Neville Street) along Middleton Road to and terminating in St. Domingo Street by a junction with the existing tramway (No. 1 of the 1882 Order). (This included the section in Oldham authorised by the Middleton Light Railways Order.)

3a. A single curve 39 yards long connecting the previous tramway with the existing tramway in Rochdale Road (No. 1 of the 1882 Order).

4. A line one mile 1,298 yards long comprising 1 mile 482 yards single and 816 yards of double track commencing in Manchester Road by a junction with the existing tramway (No. 1 of the 1878 Order), along Hollins Road and Copster Hill Road terminating in Ashton Road by a junction with the existing tramway (No. 1 of the 1882 Order).

5. A line 1,144 yards long comprising 748 yards single and 396 yards of double track commencing in Ashton Road by a junction with the existing tramway (No. 1 of the 1882 Order) along Lee Street and Union Street West terminating by a junction with the existing tramway in Union Street West (No. 11 of the 1878 Order).

6. A line 1 mile 993 yards long comprising 1 mile 223 yards single and 770 yards of double track commencing in King Street by a junction with the existing tramway (No. 1 of the 1882 Order) along Park Road, Glodwick Road and Cross Street terminating in Bottom o'th' Moor by a junction with the existing tramway (No. 1 of the 1878 Order).

7. A line 1,505 yards long comprising 1,043 yards single and 462 yards of double track commencing in Bottom o'th' Moor by a junction with the existing tramway (No. 1 of the 1878 Order) along Shaw Road terminating at the boundary with Royton at Flower Street.

8. A line 1 mile 211 yards long comprising 1,333 yards single and 638 yards of double track commencing in Mumps by a junction with the existing tramway (No. 1 of the 1878 Order) along Lees Road, terminating at the boundary with Lees.

8a. A single curve 29 yards long from Cross Street to Lees Road connecting tramways 6 and 8.

9. A line 1 mile 572 yards long comprising 1,733 yards single and 599 yards of double track commencing in Huddersfield Road by a junction with the existing tramway (No. 1 of the 1878 Order) along Ripponden Road terminating in that road.

10. A line 205 yards long comprising 117 yards single and 88 yards of double track commencing in Mumps by a junction with the existing tramway (No. 1 of the 1878 Order), easterly along a new street and Wallshaw Place terminating by a junction with the existing tramway (No. 1 of the 1878 Order) in Bottom o'th' Moor. (This was to serve the proposed depot.)

11. A double curve 44 yards long connecting the existing tramway in Featherstall Road South (No. 4 of the 1882 Order) with the existing tramway in Manchester Road (No. 1 of the 1878 Order). (This was a re-authorisation of tramway No. 5 and the southernmost 44 yards of tramway No. 4 of the 1882 Order which, had they been constructed, would have connected the horse and steam tramways.)

12. A line 552 yards long comprising 464 yards

single and 88 yards of double track commencing in Hollins Road by a junction with tramway No. 4 along Hollins Road and Hollins Road South (now Hathershaw Lane) terminating by a junction with the existing tramway (No. 1 of the 1882 Order) in Ashton Road.

No part of tramway No. 2 was to be laid in Albion Street until widened; no part of tramway No. 10 was to be laid in the new street until the street was constructed; and the Hollins Road South section of tramway No. 12 was not to be laid until road widening allowed a minimum space of 9ft 6in on each side of the track.

During the Bill's consideration by a House of Commons Committee, a petition from BET seeking running powers was rejected.

Plate 10. The photographer stands at the junction of Manchester Road and Oldham Road to record No. 38 on its way to Shaw, about 1906. *Photo, J. Maiden*

Plate 11. Probably on the same day as the previous scene, ***Plate 10***, tram No. 63 is seen in Milnrow Road heading for Werneth. *Photo, J. Maiden*

CONSTRUCTION COMMENCES

HAVING obtained its powers, Oldham wasted no time in setting about the establishment of its own electric tramway system. At the end of July the Borough Surveyor was instructed to prepare the necessary plans and the following month, following discussions with Manchester it was decided to adopt the overhead electric trolley system. Consent was sought from the two tramway companies for connections and crossings where necessary. The steam tram company readily agreed to the necessary connections provided traffic was not affected. The Carriage Company was also agreeable provided that Oldham did not operate services before the company's lease had expired - which of course was unacceptable to Oldham. The company's other conditions for the work posed no problems. As will be seen later, Oldham commenced services whilst the horse drawn trams were still running.

On 28th September, the Committee visited Liverpool to inspect the system where "a number of various types of car were to be seen". Following an invitation the Committee also visited Manchester, on 8th January 1900, to inspect the six sample cars which had been delivered (the Manchester system did not, in fact, commence operation until after Oldham!). Orders for the first cars were given on 1st February 1900 to Electric Railway & Tramway Carriage Works Limited, Preston, whose representative submitted various drawings. It was decided to buy four sample cars as the drawings supplied but fitted with air brakes. It was also decided to prepare plans for a central tramway depot at Wallshaw, Mumps. The Borough Surveyor had also been asked to produce a design for a tramcar and this was now forwarded to Hurst Nelson & Company Limited, Motherwell for a price for a sample car. However, no order resulted.

Naturally, the priority was to open the Middleton Road line, construction of which started on 6th February 1900 in Middleton Road. Work was hampered by excavations taking place simultaneously by the Gas and Water department of Oldham, as a result of which the latter department was asked to ensure that in future its work preceded that of tramways construction. It was decided that on this section the overhead would be carried by bracket arms attached to side poles, and that the Surveyors and Tramways department would supply all the electrical equipment including mains and feeders for the tramway system. This was obtained from W. T. Glover Company Limited, Trafford Park, Manchester. The Oldham Electrical Engineer, Mr. S. W. Newington, had intimated in July 1899 that he was not competent to handle the tramway electrification, and so, in July 1900, James N. Hewitt was retained as consulting electrical engineer. A temporary car shed in Neville Street adjacent to the route was supplied by A. & J. Main Company Limited, Glasgow.

A visit was made to Preston on 11th October 1900 to inspect the trams under construction before painting and finishing, and on 13th November the Committee inspected the works in Middleton Road and the temporary car shed then in course of erection. It was agreed to appoint "an experienced motor man" and a conductor; the four cars were delivered about the end of November. They were a single truck single deck car (No. 1) a single truck open top double deck car (No. 2), a bogie single deck car (No. 4) and a bogie open top double deck car (No. 3). The open top cars were fitted with reversed stairs, i.e. passengers ascended clockwise towards the extremity of the car. These were destined to be the only cars of this type in Oldham's fleet.

Plate 12. One of the bogie single-deck cars approaches the Ripponden Road junction on Huddersfied Road. Roadworks impinging on the tram track can be seen on the left-hand side. *Photo, Abel Heywood & Son*

INSPECTION AND OPENING

THE Board of Trade inspection was carried out by Lieutenant Colonel P. G. Von Donop on 6th December 1900. The line was 1,093 yards in length compared with the authorised length of 1,121 yards (tramway No. 3 of the 1899 Act) and extended from the Oldham boundary to the junction of Middleton Road and St. Domingo Street; the 28 yard shortfall presumably represented the curve into the latter street which had not then been constructed. However, the passing places had been lengthened giving 327 yards of double track compared with 264 yards authorised, but in all cases the statutory 9 feet 6 inch clearance was available. Von Donop pointed out that the line was on a falling gradient ranging down to 1 in 25 towards the Oldham boundary, the steepest section being 132 yards of 1 in 11.5. He considered the lines to be well laid but given the gradients considered it "absolutely essential" that slipper brakes should be fitted to the cars and was not prepared to recommend the Board of Trade to certify the lines as fit for passenger traffic until this had been done. Both single and double deck four wheel cars were to be worked on the line and at the time of the inspection they were fitted with hand, electrical and air brakes, the last mentioned working the same blocks as the hand brake; the cars were also equipped with Peckham lifeguards. Von Donop pointed out that Oldham had been specially warned the previous year on the matter of slipper brakes.

The official opening of the line duly took place on 15th December 1900, the deadline imposed on Oldham by the Middleton Light Railways Order. On Sundays operation was from 1.00 p.m. to 10.00 p.m. It appears that the service continued to operate without slipper brakes being fitted, prompting the Board of Trade on 4th April 1901, to instruct Oldham that no cars whatsoever, either bogie or single truck, were to be run without slipper brakes. On the 19th, Oldham informed the Board that two sets of slipper brakes were being forwarded by passenger train that evening, and eight days later confirmed that slipper brakes had been fitted. On receipt of this news the Board of Trade's Certificate as to fitness for use was issued on 2nd May. The speed was restricted to 8 miles an hour, reduced to 4 miles an hour on the descending gradient.

Had the deadline for the Middleton Road line not been met, and had it been built by the Middleton company, Oldham was empowered under the Light Railways Order to purchase it after 25 years provided it had commenced working the (then) existing tramways within the borough, the purchase price to be the cost of construction less depreciation and without any allowance for compulsory purchase; in this event Oldham was to give the company running powers.

The Middleton Electric Traction Company's service through Chadderton to the Oldham boundary did not open until 27th March 1902 following the official inspection by Major E. Druitt and Mr. A. P. Trotter on 10th March. There was a gap of a few yards between the tracks of the two systems.

Plate 13. This is the scene confronting the tram driver after turning into Ripponden Road with its double track sections and long single-track pieces.

Photo, Barrett & Company

Plate 14. Commencing in August 1903 Oldham added top covers to some of the open-top trams. Tram 58 seen here at Mumps heading for Yorkshire Street was given a cover of Oldham's own design in April 1904. *Photo, J. Valentine*

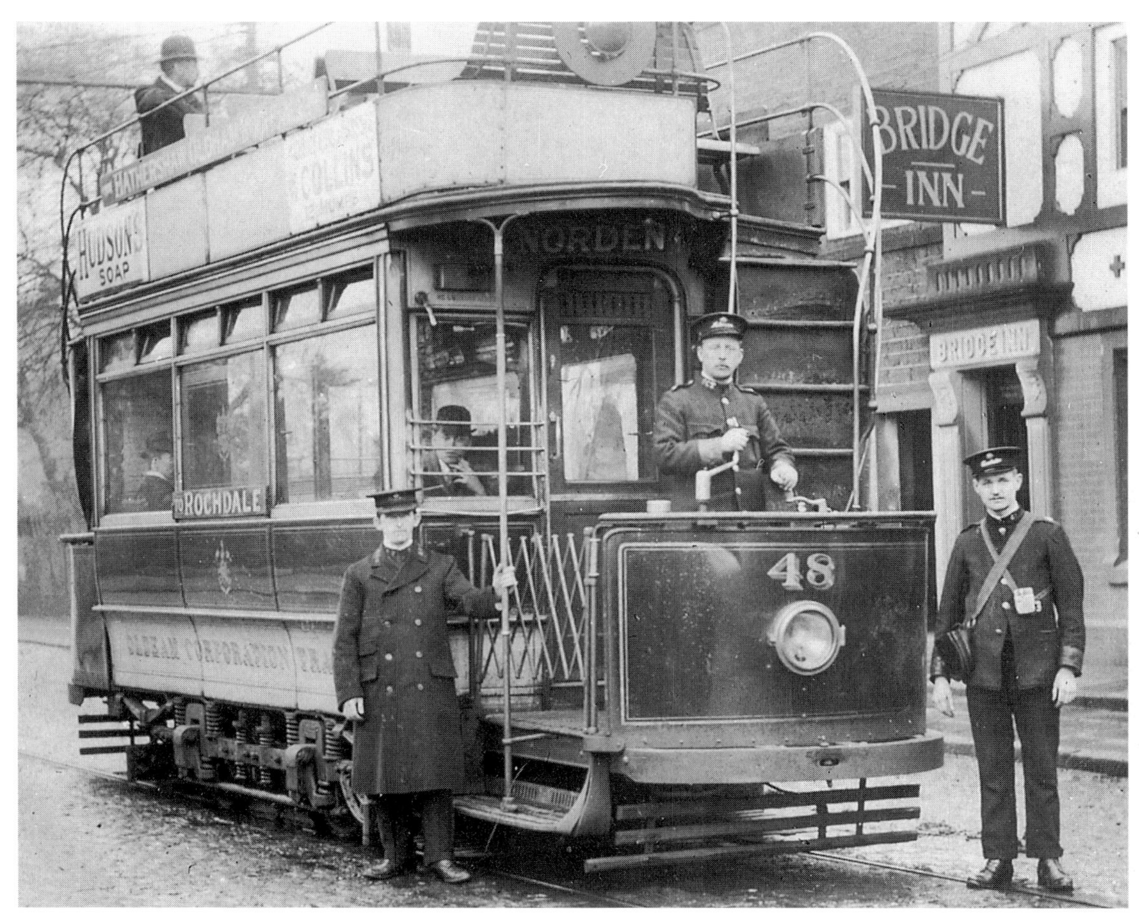

Plate 15. The jointly operated service from Hathershaw through Rochdale to Norden opened on 1st May 1906. This view shows an Oldham tram at the Norden terminus with a board at the foot of the central window reading "to Rochdale". If this was a permanent feature then presumably there was a corresponding board on the other side reading "to Oldham". The destination Norden is just visible underneath the canopy behind the driver.

Photo, Courtesy Middleton Library

MORE LINES IN OLDHAM

WITHIN two months of starting work on the Middleton Road section, construction commenced on Park Road and Glodwick Road, Hollins Road and Copster Hill Road, and Egerton Street. In February 1901 it was decided not to construct any more lines authorised by the 1899 Act until the company leases expired.

The Park Road section was inspected by Major E. Druitt, on 24th May 1901. It commenced 22 yards east of King Street at Wellington Street and continued along Glodwick Road to its junction with Lees Road, a total of 1 mile 601 yards of route of which 1,584 yards was single track. It thus represented the major part of tramway No. 6 of the 1899 Act, the overall length of which was 1 mile 993 yards, but this also included Cross Street; although included in Oldham's schedule, for some reason it was not a subject of the inspection. By deduction the shortfall of 370 yards seems on the high side for Cross Street. The inspection also covered the major part of the Lees Road tramway - No. 8 of the 1899 Act - from the middle of the first passing place near Station Street to the Oldham boundary, and which totalled 1 mile 88 yards of route compared with the overall length authorised of 1 mile 211 yards.

The inspection was accompanied by members of the Tramways Committee, using a double deck tram. It started at Station Street and then traversed Lees Road to the boundary with Lees, returning to Glodwick Road, thence along Glodwick Road and Park Road to the temporary terminal point. The inspection was completed by returning to the original starting point. By this time, J. Hewitt had been joined by Rhodes operating as Hewitt & Rhodes, consulting engineers.

Druitt reported that the Glodwick Road route curved considerably and had a continuous steep descent over 264 yards in which the steepest section was 1 in 13.8. The maximum speed permitted was 6 miles an hour, with certain sections at 4 miles an hour. He also noted that several side bracket poles in Glodwick Road were placed in the roadway which he regarded as hazardous to other traffic and suggested that they should be placed clear of the road on one side or the other.

The Lees Road tramway included 440 yards continuous gradient of which the steepest section was 1 in 13.6, with some "considerable curves" on the gradient. The maximum speed allowed on this section was 8 miles an hour with restrictions to 6 and 4 miles an hour in various places.

Druitt was informed that it was proposed to use bogie cars fitted with hand, electric and air brakes, but again he was not prepared to recommend the Board of Trade to issue the necessary Certificate for passenger traffic unless slipper brakes were used. He was not satisfied with the lifeguards fitted to the inspection car, pointing out that at one end the piston for the air brake was fitted in front of the guard and so low as to render any lifeguard useless. He would not approve this type of lifeguard and suggested that Oldham should obtain a better pattern for all its cars as soon as possible, "fixed as near as possible to the end of the car and in front of air pistons, resistance boxes and similar obstructions".

The lines were formally opened by Alderman Eckersley, the Chairman of the Tramways Committee, on Saturday, 15th June 1901, using car No. 3 which left a temporary shed off Glodwick Road at 10.30 a.m. carrying Oldham officials and Committee members. Two services were introduced, one along Park Road from its junction with Wellington Street, along Glodwick Road to its junction with Lees Road, and the other along Lees Road from Station Street to the boundary with Lees; the fare was 1*d.* (20p) in each case. The new routes were operated by three cars - the single-deckers Nos. 1 and 4 and the double-decker No. 3. They were housed in the shed located in Gargrave Street off Glodwick Road erected by J. Ashton & Sons; the line was supplied with current from the power station in Gas Street pending erection of a new power station at Greenhill, construction of which was about to commence. These cars were fitted with hand brakes for ordinary work, and electric brake and pneumatic slipper brake for emergencies.

Druitt returned to Oldham again on Thursday 18th July, this time arriving at Central Station to inspect the major part of tramway No. 4 of the 1899 Act. It extended from the first passing place in Copster Hill Road, along Copster Hill Road and Hollins Road to Gee Street on the east side of the canal bridge in Hollins Road. The inspection party travelled over this section, then returning to the starting point; the total length was 1 mile 995 yards compared with the authorised total of 1 mile 1,298 yards which extended from Manchester Road to Ashton Road. 1 mile 484 yards of the completed work was single track and Druitt noted that the proposed 164 yards of double track in Hollins Road

Plate 16. Oldham tram 49 enters the tramway centre in Rochdale from Drake Street on its way to Norden in the first year of operation of the through service. A Rochdale tram can be glimpsed on the left-hand side of the photograph.

Photo, Eclipse Series

Plate 17. Sample car No. 2 at the Waterhead terminus, showing clearly the original double-track layout with crossover at this point.

Plate 18. The opening of the jointly operated through service between Manchester and Waterhead on 21st January 1907 was handsomely celebrated.

Manchester's specially decorated tram is seen here at the Hyde Road works with some of the car works department employees. The legend at the end of the tram was "Oldham Manchester".

from Monsall Street to Copster Hill Road had been laid as single line for the time being because road improvements were still in progress; this work was completed by the end of August. Druitt commented that the lines appeared to have been very well laid and was able to recommend the Board of Trade to issue the usual Certificate for passenger traffic. The steepest gradient was noted as 1 in 13.45 and the sharpest curve as 132 yards radius. A speed of 10 miles an hour was permitted in Hollins Road from the canal bridge to Monsall Street and 8 miles an hour from there to Copster Hill Road and in Copster Hill Road.

The inspection was carried out using a single-deck car which attracted much attention in the district. Approval was given for the service to commence pending receipt of the official certificate. The Committee then repeated the trip after which the Chairman declared the line open for traffic. Initially passengers were given free rides, but later in the day a charge of 1*d.* was made. The Tramways Committee were particularly anxious to have the trams running on this section for the weekend given that on the Saturday the Hollinwood Wakes commenced. At this stage one tram was running on each of the four routes open to the public, and four more cars were expected shortly.

Druitt also noted that since his previous visit, slipper brakes had been fitted to the cars between the wheels of the bogies, activated by air pressure and applied instantaneously by the driver using a small handle, either partially or full purchase. He was also informed that Oldham was still considering which type of lifeguard to adopt in place of the type previously criticised. This was the third isolated section of tramway and was served by a small depot which was located in Copster Hill Road at the council premises.

Druitt returned to Oldham yet again (probably on 25th October) to inspect the remainder of the Hollins Road tramway some 200 yards long extending from Manchester Road to the existing track beyond the canal bridge which had been widened at a cost of £1,064. 11*s.* 4*d.*, (£51,500); there was one passing loop involved. Because of the impending reconstruction of the horse tram tracks in Manchester Road, the junction into that road had not been laid. A 6 mile per hour speed limit was imposed. It is reasonable to assume that the service was extended over the new section the same day.

Plate 19. This interesting photograph shows Manchester bogie tram 189 operating to Piccadilly and Oldham tram 42 probably operating to Waterhead at Hollinwood before the two systems were connected. The Manchester tram crew poses proudly for the photographer.

END OF HORSE AND STEAM TRACTION IN OLDHAM

THE Carriage Company's 21 year lease of the Oldham lines expired on 31st October 1901 on which date horse traction ceased. Manchester had an arrangement with the company to maintain horse tram services as far as possible while the tracks were being reconstructed for electric traction, not only in Manchester itself but also in districts such as Failsworth for which Manchester was to provide the electric services. In contrast, Oldham was now without a service on these lines until the electric service commenced. Naturally, this situation gave rise to many complaints from the public, particularly given the length of time taken to reconstruct the lines, notwithstanding the fact that as many as 900 men were employed.

The Oldham Chronicle was particularly critical on 21st December, commenting that on the tramway from Manchester to Waterhead, the portion from Hollinwood to Waterhead "was rendered useless on and from the 1st November last, by our local municipal rulers, in their wild and frantic efforts to effect and get into working order the electric tram service. Their purpose certainly was most laudable and praiseworthy, but at the same time it is proving very expensive, and annoying to the townspeople. In many cases work has been done, found out by the Corporation that it has been done in a wrong manner, then reinstated, and again recommenced, and so forth.

"For alacrity in uplifting the whole of the principal streets and thoroughfares at the centres of business and activity in Oldham our municipal rulers are to be commended, but I feel sure they will not be emulated by other towns."

In response to complaints about the absence of any service Oldham's attitude seems to have been that the Carriage Company had declined to continue operating for a further six months. The paper suggested that Oldham could have bought surplus cars and horses from the company at very attractive prices to run a service itself.

The same article referred to the tramway in Egerton Street, Radcliffe Street and Rock Street where work had started two years previously and had been finished for about eight months, but no service had been provided. It was also stated that Oldham had started work in various streets where the statutory 9 foot 6 inch clearance would not be available, without previously seeking approval of the frontagers – with expensive consequences as will be seen later.

Given the growing size of the operation the Committee decided that a separate tramways manager was appropriate and, on 27th February 1902, appointed Richard H. Wilkinson as general manager from 36 applicants at a salary of £200 (£9,400). Six were short-listed but none interviewed. Wilkinson had been appointed tramways superintendent in December 1900, having previously been assistant to the general manager of Liverpool Corporation Tramways.

The B.R.O. lease had also expired on 31st October but the company had agreed to continue working along Rochdale Road as far as West Street at a rental of £4 a week provided it was given ten days' notice of final cessation. A week later arrangements were made for the company to operate on the Featherstall Road route; at the end of January 1902 the company threatened to cease operating Featherstall Road over the question of rates payable. The steam trams finally ceased on 28th June. It was thus then possible to go ahead with the reconstruction of the remainder of the steam tram tracks as well.

Plate 20. Manchester tram number 398 halts in Market Place on its way to Manchester about 1909. The facing crossover seen to the rear of the tram gave access to the single curve leading into Henshaw Street for trams operating to Chadderton Road. *Photo, J. Valentine*

Plate 21. This view is thought to show tram 63, the first Oldham tram to be fitted with a balcony type top cover incorporating extended upper deck, in December 1909. *Photo, Light Railway & Tramway Journal*

Plate 22. An interesting view showing painting of the poles and bracket arms in Lees Road. *Photo, Courtesy N. Ellis*

CONSTRUCTION PROBLEMS

RETURNING to November 1901, Oldham had decided to relay the steam tram tracks in St. Domingo Street, King Street and Ashton Road, which were mainly single track with passing loops, as double track. The Town Clerk pointed out that notices would have to be served on the frontagers where the distance between the nearest rail and the pavement would be less than 9ft. 6ins. The Board of Trade, which had been consulted on the matter, said that it had no objection on engineering grounds to the proposed doubling but its view was expressed without prejudice to the rights of the frontagers under Section 34 of the 1899 Oldham Act.

On 11th December, the Committee inspected the Wallshaw Depot then under construction and also visited the various works on track reconstruction in Huddersfield Road, Union Street, Ashton Road, Manchester Street, King Street and St. Domingo Street. As a result visits were paid to Askham Brothers & Wilson, and Hadfields, Sheffield to urge the firms to expedite the delivery of crossings and points which were urgently required. It was suggested that one track from Hollinwood to the Black Horse Hotel at Werneth should be completed as soon as possible so that cars could be run over this particular section.

The double track in St. Domingo Street was completed by January 1902, and in the following month an injunction against Oldham was sought by frontagers in the Chancery Court of the Palatine of Lancaster.

On 7th March Druitt inspected the tracks in St. Domingo Street, King Street and Ashton Road which commenced with a junction with the Middleton Road tramway and ended in a junction with the Copster Hill Road tramway. The Oldham Evening Chronicle said that "Inspections of the Oldham tramway routes have not been so frequent recently as to have lost the charm of novelty" and noted that a good number of spectators watched the proceedings. Druitt arrived in Oldham at 9.30 a.m. and departed from Central station at 10.30. During the intervening hour the party, which included the newly appointed manager, boarded a double-deck tram at Copster Hill and ran over the route to Middleton Road then returning in one of the single-deck cars to Copster Hill and back again to Park Road. At Copster Hill "a demonstration of the valuable device used to ensure safety if a telephone or other wire falls across the trolley wire was given with success".

As noted earlier, this stretch had been reconstructed as double track throughout replacing the previous single line and passing loops used by the steam trams, the overall length being 1,228 yards. The inspector pointed out that in a "great many places" there was not a 9ft. 6in. clearance between the kerb and the nearest rail. All frontagers' objections had been met in Ashton Road and King Street "but in St. Domingo Street, I was informed that consent of all the frontagers had not yet been obtained, so, until this is settled, I cannot recommend the Board of Trade to sanction that short piece of line in St. Domingo Street". He was able to report that the whole line had been well laid and imposed speed limits of 6 miles an hour in Ashton Road, 8 miles an hour in King Street and 4 miles an hour in St. Domingo Street. Compulsory stops were required before crossing Lee Street, Union Street and Manchester Street.

The portion from Star Inn (Union Street) to Copster Hill Road was opened on the morning of Wednesday 12th March. Alderman Chadwick, who had succeeded Alderman Eckersley as Chairman of the Tramways Committee on 21st November, 1901, drove the first car along the route and on returning to the Star Inn "delivered a short address to a large assembly". The new section linked up with the portion already operating from Hollinwood which was divided into two penny stages from the junction of Hollins Road and Copster Hill Road. Two days later the property owners who had commenced proceedings against Oldham agreed to suspend the action on condition that within two months the St. Domingo Street lines were reconstructed to leave at least 9ft. 6in. between the edge of the footpath and the nearest line of rails, which implied replacement of the double track by a single track. At this time the men who were working on tramway construction in the evenings and on Sunday decided to go on strike because they received the same pay as those operating in the daytime, which was in fact the basis on which the work had been commenced. At the weekend Oldham introduced workmen's cars on the various routes from 5.10 a.m. and commenced operation on Sundays at the earlier time of 9.30 a.m., finishing at the later time of 11.00 p.m. It was reported that many people watched the new cars in the morning and afternoon: "They have an excellent appearance and the comments made on the general effect by the groups of bystanders were for the most part very favourable in character. "It has been noticed however by the congregations of the places of worship passed on the King Street and Ashton Road routes that the cars cause considerable disturbance and interfere to no slight degree with the quietude of the service. This was particularly apparent when the cars passed in couples, the building being shaken by their impetus and weight".

At the council meeting on 2nd April 1902, Councillor Sixsmith asked if the Chairman would be prepared to tell the Board of Trade Inspector everything regarding the St. Domingo Street section.

"A double track had been laid without any power to do so, without any money to do it, and without permission to borrow the money for doing the work. It was a most remarkable proceeding."

In reply, the Chairman of the Surveyor's & Tramways Committee, Alderman Chadwick, said the post "required the meekness of Moses, the craft of Jacob, the wisdom of Solomon, the patience of Job, the eloquence of Paul and the courage of Peter. More than that he had to be capable of working miracles in a snowstorm, or making extreme preparations for a football match".

St. Domingo Street, now relaid with single track, and thus meeting the frontagers' objections, was brought into use when the Copster Hill Road service was extended to Middleton Road, possibly on 19th April.

Druitt's inspection of the 130 yard replacement single track in St. Domingo Street took place on the morning of 1st May 1902 when a speed limit of 4 miles an hour was imposed. On this visit he also inspected 140 yards of double track in Manchester Road running from a junction with the Hollins Road line to the Oldham boundary with Failsworth at Hollinwood, allowing an 8 mile an hour speed limit. Lastly, he covered the remaining length of Ashton Road from Copster Hill Road to the boundary comprising 1,330 yards of double track, allowing a speed limit of 10 miles an hour. An increase to 12 miles an hour in Ashton Road between Broadway Street and the boundary was allowed provided a satisfactory speed indicator was provided in the trams. Following representations he increased the speed limit in King Street between Primrose Bank and Union Street from 8 to 10 miles an hour. Oldham decided to inform the Board of Trade that it was not proposed to install speed indicators nor to run the cars faster than 10 miles an hour. A service between Hathershaw and Middleton Road was introduced, possibly on 9th June. At this time, it was not possible to operate more than 35 trams because of the limited power supply, pending the commissioning of Greenhill.

The Oldham, Ashton and Hyde Electric Tramway Limited, a BET company, had commenced a service of electric cars to the Oldham boundary at Hathershaw (Fir Tree Avenue) on 12th June, 1899, under powers granted by the Oldham, Ashton-under-Lyne, Hyde and District Electric Tramways Order 1896, confirmed by the Tramways Order Confirmation (No. 2) Act 1896. Proposed lines in Oldham had been struck out of the Bill following an objection from Oldham. In February, 1903 after refusing an approach in December, 1902, Oldham agreed to the company attaching its overhead to the Oldham terminal pole, subject to a yearly payment.

Plate 23. This view, probably taken about 1913, shows tram 36 awaiting departure from the Hollinwood terminus for Lees, and in the background the imposing frontage of the Hollinwood depot. Regrettably this building was demolished in 1994.

FORMAL OPENING OF THE SYSTEM

THE reconstruction of the former horse tram tracks was also not without its problems. An action against Oldham over the margin in Manchester Road was settled only when Oldham agreed to obtain the width required by setting back the wall of Werneth Park. The reconstruction of this main route through the town from the boundary of Oldham with Failsworth to its boundary at Waterhead with Springhead Urban District on Huddersfield Road via Yorkshire Street, and the alternative route via Union Street, represented the biggest single tramway project.

However, all was ready by 16th May when Druitt carried out his inspection. This covered the former horse tram route commencing at Hollins Road, along Manchester Road, Market Place, High Street, Yorkshire Street, Mumps, Bottom o'th' Moor and Huddersfield Road to the Oldham boundary, Union Street, and the short section of Lees Road joining up with the existing tramway in that thoroughfare. The first tramway was mainly double track apart from some single sections and interlaced track in Yorkshire Street; Union Street was 990 yards of double track and the Lees Road piece was also double. Speed limits were generally 8 or 10 miles an hour but with some sections at 6 and 4 miles an hour. Druitt noted that the bases around the centre poles in Union Street had not then been fixed in position but "are to be at once". He said they should be rounded off to prevent people standing on them between the poles and the car. On the Lees Road section he required the trolleywires under the railway bridge to be moved to the side so that they did not come "exactly over the car as the bridge is rather low, and a person standing up could touch the wire". Naturally, Oldham agreed to make this alteration. The inspector added: "Also it would be well if the trolley wire under the railway bridge in Mumps were protected at the sides by wooden battens to render it less likely to be touched by people standing up on the car. The usual notices should be posted up on both sides of the bridge calling attention to the danger of touching the trolley wire."

Public services commenced on 17th May 1902, and the formal opening took place on Whit Monday, 19th May. Eight cars "gaily decorated with choice flowers, ferns, Union Jacks and other flags" conveyed members of the Corporation and invited guests from the Town Hall by way of High Street and Manchester Road to Hollinwood, the first car leaving at 11.05 a.m. The wife of the Tramways Committee Chairman, Mrs. H. Chadwick, started the first car and Mrs. J. A. Hanson, the Deputy Chairman's wife, the second. From Hollinwood, the party journeyed by Hollins Road, Ashton Road and Union Street to Waterhead. Councillor J. A. Hanson formally declared the route open to the public at both Hollinwood and Waterhead. The party then returned to the newly constructed tram depot at Wallshaw, where the Mayor, Councillor J. Eckersley, unveiled a marble tablet commemorating the event and expressed his pleasure at performing such a ceremony. He said that the Tramways Committee had worked very hard and trusted that their efforts would be crowned with success. He recalled the time when the tram service from Hollinwood to Waterhead cost 6*d.*, subsequently reduced to 4*d.*, but now Oldham offered greater facilities and the fare was still less at 3*d.* (59p). Alderman Chadwick then formally opened the car depot. The assembled company was then photographed before returning to the Town Hall, the whole proceedings having taken about an hour and a half. Over lunch there were "various congratulatory speeches".

It is appropriate at this stage to give some details of the tramways themselves. The track construction, building of depots – permanent and temporary – erection of standards, overhead equipment, and cables was designed and carried out by the Borough Engineer Mr. S. A. Pickering and his assistant Mr. H. Clegg; Hewitt and Rhodes acted as consulting electrical engineers for the overhead equipment. The track was constructed by Oldham, electrical equipment was supplied by W. T. Glover & Company Limited, Manchester. Barrow Haematite Steel Company Limited supplied 2,000 tons of rails to March 1901 and a subsequent order for 3,000 tons was given to Dick, Kerr & Co. Ltd., who had supplied 2,000 tons by the time of the official opening; both firms also supplied fish plates. The special track work comprising points and crossings was supplied by Askham Brothers and Wilson Limited, Sheffield and the rolling stock by the Electric Railway & Tramway Carriage Company Limited, Preston. The car depot was constructed by Edward Stephenson, Oldham.

The rails were to a special section weighing 100 lb. a yard but the head of the Dick, Kerr rail was about a ¼ inch wider than that of the Barrow Company. The tie bars were supplied by Askham

Brothers and Wilson Limited and fixed at 9 feet intervals. At that time there were 32 double junctions in the system besides the various passing places, turnouts and the special work at the Wallshaw car depot, all of which apart from those at the depot were supplied by Askham Brothers and Wilson Limited. At the time of the opening 183 pairs of points and 279 crossings had been used in the track.

The track bed was prepared to a depth of 13 inches below the finished level; the rails were then laid upon old setts placed at intervals of about 15 feet, to a gauge of 4 feet 8½ inches. When the rails were satisfactorily laid, six inches of concrete was laid to a width of eight feet for single track and 13 feet 6 inches for double track. The road surface comprised six inch granite sets paved on a bed of sand 1½ inches thick, the finished surface being about ½ inch higher than the tread of the rail. The steepest gradient on the system, including lines not then constructed, was the Middleton Road section previously mentioned.

The electrical network comprised five feeder cables of various lengths with cross sections from 0.75 square inches to 0.1 square inches. The system had 25 feed points and 45 section boxes. The overhead trolley wire was 3/0 gauge and double throughout the system fixed at 22 feet 3 inches above the carriageway. The wire was manufactured by Frederick Smith & Sons, Anaconda Works, Salford, with overhead fittings mostly supplied by Estler Brothers.

The Wallshaw car depot was approximately 111 yards by 35 yards with 25 foot headroom constructed to accommodate 70 cars on eight tracks. These converged into one track to the running line entailing 44 points and 22 crossings. The rails were fixed to brick piers, 1 feet 6 inches square and 5 feet 6 inches high, built at 9 feet centres thus providing a pit over the entire depot area. The depot also included four workshops.

The electrification of the former horse tram tracks enabled the Park Road and Glodwick Road service to be converted into a continuous "circular" route by extending it along Union Street and King Street; this probably commenced on 22nd May rather than 22nd March as stated in the annual reports. On the same day the service from the boundary on Lees Road to Station Street was extended through the town to Market Place being further extended on 9th June to Hollinwood via Werneth. On this date also, the Middleton Road–Hollins Road and Hathershaw–Star Inn services were combined to form a route running between Hathershaw and Middleton Road.

An unusual accident happened on 14th June 1902, at Mumps. Whilst the conductor was collecting the fares on the top deck, he left a young man to attend to the trolley rope. For some reason the trolley came off the wire and he was unable to replace it. It became entangled with the other wires and the young man was lifted into the air and subsequently thrown to the ground. As the trolley fell back it caught two passengers on the top deck who were thrown from their seats to the pavement suffering superficial injuries requiring hospital treatment.

Plate 24. Milnrow Road, Shaw, at Beal Lane (Four Lane Ends) with car No. 80 awaiting departure for Werneth. It appears that the conductor is on the platform.
Photo, John Schofield

MORE OPENINGS

ON 29th August, Druitt carried out more inspections, namely Shaw Road (tramway No. 7 of the 1899 Act) running from Huddersfield Road to the boundary with Royton; the branch from this along Egerton Street, Radcliffe Street and Rock Street, terminating at the intersection with Lord Street, representing most of tramway No. 2 of the same Act; and the reconstructed former steam tramway along Rochdale Road from Middleton Road to the boundary with Royton.

The Oldham Evening Chronicle commented that the inspector "must by this time have obtained a fair knowledge of the contours of the Oldham district" given his various inspections and tours on the different routes. Druitt arrived at the Central station and inspection commenced shortly after 10.30 a.m. from Union Street. Using a double-deck car, the inspector and accompanying officials travelled first along Rochdale Road to Boundary Street returning to the Star Inn thence along Union Street and Shaw Road to Flower Street, Higginshaw; on the return the car travelled over Egerton Street, Radcliffe Street and Rock Street to Lord Street thence returning via Shaw Road, Cross Street, Lees Road and Mumps to the Town Hall arriving there about 12.40 p.m.

The paper noted that "speaking generally, the trip was of a satisfactory character, although a few minor contretemps happened that could well have been dispensed with in the presence of the inspector". There was a short stop in Rochdale Road while workmen were using the tower wagon to adjust the overhead wiring; near the Egerton Arms the car left the rails "and a somewhat lengthy stoppage ensued until it was put on the track again". Two or three times during the journey, as under Mumps Bridge, the trolley left the wire.

Regarding the sharp turns from Egerton Street into Radcliffe Street and from Radcliffe Street into Rock Street the Chronicle noted that

"There had been some feeling of apprehension as to this particular portion of the route, certainly justified by the element of danger caused by the difficulties of the situation. The corners were negotiated, both going and returning, very successfully, but the car was driven with great care. There is not the slightest doubt that this part will always have to be run over with extreme caution."

Tramway No. 2 would have met the Henshaw Street line (then under construction) end-on but the Albion Street section had not been constructed because the street had not been widened as required by the Act; as built the line was 1,008 yards long (1,122 yards authorised) and included 676 yards of single track. A 4 mile an hour speed limit was imposed apart from 10 miles an hour in Egerton Street between the passing loops. Druitt mentioned that the points of the passing loop at St. Stephen's Street required adjusting as a car was liable to be de-railed there. The speed limit in Shaw Road - 1,505 yards of route - was generally 8 miles an hour; the speed limit in Rochdale Road was also 8 miles an hour. Rochdale Road was 1,625 yards long and included 1,228 yards of double track.

Although not mentioned in his report, it is possible that Druitt's inspection also included Cross Street; if not, then presumably it was included in the inspection of the main route and the short portion of Lees Road on 16th May, but again if this were the case, it was not mentioned in the inspection report.

The Inspector's requirements having been met, further service changes were introduced on 30th August. The Hathershaw and Middleton Road (Chadderton boundary) service was curtailed to operate between King Street (Star Inn) and Chadderton boundary, but a service was introduced from Hathershaw to the Royton boundary along Rochdale Road. Also, a cross town service was introduced between Middleton Road and Higginshaw (Shaw Road) via Park Road and Cross Street.

A service between Higginshaw and Lord Street (Rock Street) opened on 4th September 1902, the delay resulting from a shortage of trams. As early as the following February there were complaints from the occupiers of property in Rock Street and Radcliffe Street that the lines had not been laid in accordance with the published plans. Oldham's reaction was to ask whether the objectors would accept payment so that Oldham could continue to operate or, alternatively, Oldham would purchase the properties concerned. The property owners were not prepared to agree terms and insisted on the lines being relaid in accordance with the Parliamentary plans. Oldham's reaction was to remove some of the rails at the Rock Street - Radcliffe Street junction. It is not clear whether the track was relaid in accordance with the plans or whether the service continued in truncated form. However, in October it was decided to discontinue operation on Thursdays. Eventually, on 17th April

1904, the service ceased completely; 86 yards of track was removed from this section.

The end of August 1902, marked the commissioning of Greenhill Power Station when two 600 hp generators solely for traction purposes came on stream. Two more generators of 1,300 hp each were also being installed. The current generated was taken by a newly laid cable along Waterloo Street and Gas Street to the Rhodes Bank station which for the time being was to distribute all the energy required. The official opening took place on 29th June 1903.

On his next visit on Thursday 16th October, Druitt inspected tramways Nos. 1 and 9 of the 1899 Act. The former, commencing in Market Place by a junction with the existing tracks was via Henshaw Street, Barker Street and Chadderton Road to the Oldham boundary in that road. It was single track with passing loops with an overall length of 1,601 yards and 988 yards of passing loops. The speed limit was generally 8 miles an hour. The other line was also single track with passing loops, an overall length of 1 mile 582 yards including 1,631 yards of single track, running along Ripponden Road from a junction with the existing tramway in Huddersfield Road and terminating 40 yards beyond the Moorside Hotel; the speed limit here was generally 10 miles an hour.

The Ripponden Road route was opened on 18th October with services operating from Moorside to Market Place via Union Street, and from Hill Stores (Ripponden Road) to Hollinwood via Union Street and Hollins Road. On the same day a service commenced between Lees Brook (Lees boundary) and the Chadderton boundary over the newly constructed Chadderton Road; with these new routes the former service from Lees Brook to Hollinwood was discontinued. It must be said that this last mentioned route was a less sensible cross town route than the new introductions.

Druitt's next visit was on 14th November to inspect the former steam tramway in Featherstall Road North and Featherstall Road South, and the connection of this (tramway No. 11 of the 1899 Act) to the existing tramway in Manchester Road. The total length was 1 mile 378 yards of which 1,329 yards was single. The speed limit was 8 miles an hour between passing loops except on the curves into Rochdale Road which were restricted to 4 miles an hour. A service was introduced on 19th November from Manchester Road, Werneth (fire station) along the Featherstall Roads and Rochdale Road to the boundary with Royton.

On 6th February 1903, Druitt reported on an inspection of the reconstructed tramway in Union Street West and an extension of this as far as Lee Street representing part of tramway No. 5 of the 1899 Act. This was single track with passing loops, 540 yards in total; he imposed a speed limit of 8 miles an hour, 4 miles an hour at points. The borough surveyor had been instructed to construct tramway No. 5, which included Lee Street to its junction with Ashton Road, in January 1901; second thoughts had evidently prevailed, but not before the complex junction to Ashton Road, crossing Copster Hill Road, had been laid.

Druitt also approved a single curve from Henshaw Street to Market Place which had replaced a double curve inspected on 16th October 1902; the double curve led to objections from the frontagers because the clearance from the kerb was less than 9ft. 6in. Oldham seems to have anticipated the outcome of this inspection for a service was introduced between Union Street West and Higginshaw on 11th December 1902, replacing the service between Middleton Road and Higginshaw; at the same time, the Middleton Road (Chadderton boundary) and Star Inn service was extended to Wellington Street (King Street).

On 17th January 1903 the Lees Road and Chadderton Road through service ceased in favour of Lees Road (Lees boundary) and Werneth fire station, and Chadderton Road (Chadderton boundary) to Market Place.

Plate 25. A busy scene – also at Beal Lane – shows top covered car 75, possibly waiting to reverse, and single deck car 21 bound for Werneth. *Photo, J. E. Preston*

FINAL OPERATION BY THE CARRIAGE COMPANY

IT is appropriate at this stage to mention that the Manchester Carriage & Tramways Company finally ceased operating on 31st March 1903. The last services operated by the company were from Manchester to the Oldham boundary at Hollinwood via Oldham Road and to Ashton via Ashton Old Road and Ashton New Road, and between Ashton and Stalybridge. Manchester introduced electric services to Hollinwood and to the Ashton boundary the next day. Horse trams were operated on a temporary basis in Ashton and Stalybridge during reconstruction but these facilities were provided by Manchester. The possibility now existed for through transport by electric tram between Oldham and Manchester but it was to be another four years before this facility was introduced.

It was however possible to reach Oldham by electric tram from Manchester before the electrification to Hollinwood, via Middleton or via Denton, both of which were served by Manchester Corporation trams. On 24th March, a correspondent of the Manchester Evening Chronicle made a circular tram tour, outwards via Middleton, and referred to the Oldham section in these terms:

"...but we must allow the Middleton Electric Traction Company the unconscious honour of transporting us to Oldham – in a long one-storey car with a few open seats at each end. The Oldham Corporation undertakes the great responsibility of our conveyance from the outskirts into the centre of the town for the sum of one penny. It has to be confessed that 'Owdham' is not a thing of beauty and a joy forever. But its appetite for cotton is prodigious. The 12 million spindles of its nearly 300 mills are said to eat up one fifth of all the cotton imported from abroad. If the animated talk of be-shawled mill hands, the ceaseless clatter of countless clogs, the level-headedness of typical Lancastrians interest us, we are interested now. The houses are smoke-blackened and the atmosphere is smoke-laden, but you do not go to Oldham for scenery. Its streets teem with life, and therefore with a kind of attractiveness. Man in the mass has an interest that man in the individual has not, and you see him in a mass of tolerable extent at Oldham. Mix with the crowd; wander past the shops, saunter through the market, stroll down the dingy by-ways. If you would know humanity you must know Lancashire; if you would know Lancashire you must know Oldham. It is only a nodding acquaintance, though, that we can form this afternoon. A Corporation tram takes us through Hathershaw, and one of the Oldham, Ashton and Hyde Electric Tramway cars carries us on to Ashton-under-Lyne."

Plate 26. One boy holds a cricket bat and other bystanders watch the photographer taking this view of car 30 on its way to Shaw, seen in Oldham Road, Shaw.

Photo, John Schofield

FINANCIAL MATTERS

FOR some twelve months it had been apparent that the cost of constructing the tramways had exceeded estimates and was, in fact, in excess of the borrowing powers which had been granted. The borough Auditor was called in to examine the situation. Working under great pressure and at some cost to the efficiency of his own department he duly produced details of where the extra costs had been incurred. It was estimated that constructing double instead of single track in various places accounted for £57,862. It was however apparent that there was little if any effective control over the supply and usage of materials in the surveyor's department and detailed proposals were put forward for appropriate systems to be instituted. The outcome of the investigations was that the Borough Surveyor was invited to resign, which he refused to do. He was given three months' notice expiring on 21st July 1903. He was succeeded on 30th July by the assistant borough surveyor, who was appointed without the post being advertised.

The surveyor's department was reorganised and the council applied to the Board of Trade for additional borrowing powers amounting to £100,053 (£4.7m). The Board approved £78,969 (£3.7m) comprising £61,992 (£2.9m) for permanent way work and street widening necessitated by tramways and £16,977 (£0.8m) for electrical equipment, but disallowed the balance of £21,084 (£1.0m) which had been expended in repairing the main highways.

At the council meeting in May 1903, it was suggested that Oldham had been paying 4.5% interest on bank borrowings compared with the usual 3.5% on authorised borrowings. It was also suggested that the tramways had lost £10,000 (£470,000) in the twelve months to March; the accounts subsequently showed a loss of £7,715 (£360,000).

As a result, economy measures were introduced on 18th May so that the revised services could be operated by 42 trams instead of 56, with a reduction in employment of 30 saving about £40 (£1,900) in wages and £80 (£3,800) in electricity each week. The reductions were mainly in the all day services. As from 18th May the Middleton Road and Wellington Street service was curtailed to operate (as previously) between Middleton Road and Star Inn, extended to Park Gates as traffic required. The Moorside and Market Place and the Ripponden Road (Hill Stores) and Hollinwood services were replaced by one operating between Moorside and Hollinwood (via Union Street).

At this time a long running dispute between Manchester and Salford about the terms for Salford cars to run over Manchester tracks was being resolved. Under the settlement, Salford extended its area of operation, but had insufficient trams to operate the new services. Oldham offered cars on loan, but Salford opted to hire 16 from Manchester, for services which commenced on 31st May.

In the following month, the Oldham coroner sued Oldham tramways for £16. 14*s.* 0*d.* (£790) damages caused to his brougham in a collision with a tram. He lost the case and was made to pay the costs.

Plate 27. High Street, Shaw, showing one of the early top covered cars.

Photo, J. Maiden

Plate 28. The photographer's main interest was the Grand Theatre in King Street but fortunately his view also included Oldham's tram No. 3. This was the undertaking's only bogie double decker and featured reversed stairs, i.e. passengers ascended clockwise to the extremity of the car. The view dates from just before the first World War and the car is on its way to Royton. *Photo, J. L. Brown*

Plate 29. A contrast in gradients showing on the right the climb up Manchester Road towards Market Place and on the left the descent along Featherstall Road South to Werneth station.
Photo, Abel Heywood & Son

Plate 30. A Rochdale tram, possibly number 63, at that system's New Hey terminus. The service to this point opened on 1st March 1912 which was one mile 795 yards from the Oldham terminus at Shaw. A link joining the two systems was first proposed in July 1911 and eventually accepted by Oldham in April 1918. However, it was not built but tramway connection between the two districts will be made when the railway between Oldham and Rochdale is converted to Metrolink operation.
Photo, Whitworth's Series

LEES TRAMWAYS

ON 12th September 1901 Oldham received a deputation from Lees which had previously suggested the extension of the Oldham system to Lees. Lees wished to provide the track and equipment whilst Oldham would provide the power and take a lease of the lines at a rental which would give "a fair compensation to the Urban Authority for the capital expended and interest thereon". Lees reminded Oldham that there were other proposals before the Lees council at that time from a syndicate proposing a line from Lees Brook through Lees to Waterhead with a loop line from the Swan Inn round by Hey and Crossbank; these lines formed a small part of a scheme for tramways in Springhead and Saddleworth. Lees wanted to know whether, if it approved the syndicate proposals, Oldham would be willing to grant the syndicate powers to run its cars on Oldham lines or run its cars on the syndicate lines. Oldham pointed out that it had already decided against granting running powers over its lines to any other operator. Oldham was then asked if it would run over the lines of the syndicate on the loop and round by Waterhead, Lees pointing out that the district was so small that it would not pay to lay the lines itself. Lees would not entertain the syndicate proposals unless terms were arranged with Oldham for running powers. Oldham made it clear to Lees that it would not deal with the syndicate as far as Lees was concerned and that any agreement had to be made absolutely and entirely between Lees and Oldham. Lees pointed out that it had never made any proposals to the syndicate; the latter had always approached Lees. The Lees representatives considered Lees part of Oldham and had hoped that Oldham would take action to incorporate it within the borough. The outcome of the meeting was that Lees would put detailed proposals for tramways to Oldham including estimated costs; Oldham for its part agreed in principle that Lees would lay the lines and that Oldham would work them subject to suitable terms and arrangements for the completion of the scheme. Negotiations resulted in agreed terms on 23rd October 1902.

Powers for the construction of tramways were duly conferred by the Lees Urban District Council Tramways Order 1902. The lines authorised were:

1. A continuation of tramway No. 8 of the Oldham 1899 Act, 641 yards long comprising 338 yards of single track and 303 yards of double track along High Street from the boundary with Oldham to the boundary with Springhead Urban District. There were double track sections at each end of the line and an intermediate passing loop of 66 yards.
2. A single line 96 yards long commencing in High Street by a junction with tramway No. 1, along Elliott Street and St. John Street.
3. A line 631 yards long comprising 268 yards single and 363 yards of double track commencing in High Street by a junction with tramway No. 1, along High Street and St. John Street terminating at the boundary with the Parish of Cross Bank. The line commenced single and then became double.
4. A single line 17 yards long connecting tramways Nos. 1 and 3.

Lees wanted Oldham to construct the lines but it lacked the powers to do so and in March 1903 suggested that Lees should advertise for tenders, one of the conditions of the contract being that the contractor should purchase materials from Oldham stocks as far as possible.

Work commenced on the Lees extension, the first beyond the Oldham boundary, on 15th June. It was a fairly short extension and was inspected by Druitt on 31st July. He arrived at Mumps via Rochdale "by Lancashire and Yorkshire Special" and was met by Mr. Hewitt of Hewitt & Rhodes, the engineers. The party, which included the Oldham manager, journeyed to the Oldham–Lees boundary at Lees Brook. The Oldham Evening Chronicle reported that the villagers had displayed considerable interest in the undertaking and many were looking out for the official inspection and "hoping that no obstacle would intervene to prevent the new roadway being opened for the wakes tomorrow". The inspection was by open top tram. The journey to County End and back "proceeded with perfect smoothness".

Druitt reported that it was part of tramway No. 1 of the 1902 Order, a single track line with passing loops which he recorded as 684 yards in length despite the fact that the authorisation of the whole line was for 641 yards! 362 yards of it was single track. The speed limit was generally 8 miles an hour. Druitt noted that the line was to be worked by Oldham and that its cars had slipper brakes - "which are necessary on this line". The official opening took place the following morning at 11.00 a.m. when Councillor Shaw declared the tramway to be open for use. The service from Hollinwood via Market Place was extended over the Lees tracks. The other authorised lines in Lees were not built.

Although the general terms of Oldham's lease of the Lees Tramways had been agreed in October 1902, the lease itself was not executed until 1st June 1905, covering the 21 year period from inspection to 31st July 1924. The yearly rental was £376. 4*s.* 6*d.* payable half-yearly and in addition Oldham paid all rates and taxes (except Income Tax). Oldham was to provide the electricity and work the tramways as part of the general tramways system and was not allowed to assign or underlet without written consent.

Generally the service was to be at least 20 minutes frequency with a 30 minute frequency at quieter periods and on Sundays. Workmen's cars were to be run at convenient hours at fares not exceeding ½*d.* per mile. Oldham was to work the tramways so as to cause the least possible wear and tear and was responsible for maintenance, repair, and renewal as necessary including the 18 inch margin on either side. At the end of the lease the tramways and road were to be in good repair and condition, reasonable wear and tear caused by operating the tramway accepted. In return, Oldham was given the exclusive use of the tramway and Lees undertook not to grant a lease to any other body on any further tramways which might be constructed in the district. If any additional lines were constructed, Oldham was to be given a six month option to lease them, on agreed terms or otherwise as settled by the Board of Trade.

The route from Chadderton Road to Market Place was extended to Higginshaw, this change taking place on 24th August 1903. On 14th December, a further change took place when the service between Union Street West and Higginshaw was revised to operate between Union Street West and Waterhead. However, it did not last long in this form, being curtailed to operate between Lee Street (Union Street West) and Mumps Bridge on 13th June 1904.

Plate 31. Mumps showing a car bound for Hollinwood, about 1927. *Photo, Lilywhite Ltd*

LINES IN ROYTON AND CROMPTON

AT the turn of the century Royton and Crompton were working closely together over tramway developments in the districts. Royton had the steam tramway service along the main road by virtue of its strategic position between Rochdale and Oldham whereas Crompton had none. In fact, Crompton had access to Oldham only through Royton, hence the co-operation. The discussions resulted in the appointment by both councils of Reginald P. Wilson as consulting engineer on 15th October 1900. Wilson's responsibilities were to draw up plans for tramways in the districts, obtain Parliamentary powers, and arrange for subsequent construction. At that time the councils seem to have had open minds as to whether to operate the lines themselves or lease to a company or Oldham; BET expressed interest in taking a lease. Both districts obtained powers in 1901. The Royton Urban District Council Tramways Order 1901 confirmed by the Tramways Orders Confirmation (No. 2) Act, 1901 authorised the following lines:

1. A line 1 mile 97 yards long comprising 1,472 yards single and 385 yards of double track commencing by a junction with the existing tramway in Oldham Road (tramway No. 29 of the Manchester, Bury, and Rochdale Tramways (Extensions) Order, 1882) along Shaw Road to the boundary with Crompton. The double track comprised 77 yard lengths at the beginning and end of the tramway with three intermediate passing loops each 77 yards long.

1a. A double curve 29 yards long from Oldham Road to Shaw Road.

2. A line 1,544 yards long comprising 528 yards single and 1,016 yards of double track from the boundary with Oldham along Higginshaw Lane and Heyside to the boundary with Crompton. There were two passing loops, each of 77 yards, and a double track section of 862 yards ending 18 yards from the Crompton boundary. The line represented a continuation of tramway no 7 of the 1899 Oldham Act.

3. A line 1 mile 82 yards long comprising 1,136 yards single and 706 yards of double track commencing by a junction with the existing tramway (tramway No. 29 of the Manchester, Bury, and Rochdale Tramways (Extensions) Order, 1882) in Rochdale Road near Kershaw Street and terminating in Rochdale Road at the boundary with Rochdale. This line replaced roughly the southern half of tramway No. 26 of the 1882 Extensions Order, a 3ft. 6in. gauge line 2 miles 114 yards long. The double track comprised passing places 156, 88, 385 and 77 yards long from south to north along the line.

3a. A single line 44 yards long commencing by a junction with tramway No. 3, along Dogford Road to the car sheds of the steam tramway.

3b. A single curve 26 yards long connecting tramways No. 3 and 3a.

Until the purchase of the steam tramways, Royton was not allowed to construct junctions or otherwise interfere with the tramways in Rochdale Road, Oldham Road and Dogford Road except with the previous written consent of the tramway company.

Similarly, in the same session of Parliament, the Crompton Urban District Council Tramways Order 1901 was also confirmed by the Tramways Orders Confirmation (No. 2) Act, 1901. The lines authorised were:

1. A continuation of Tramway No. 1 of the Royton Order, 1,646 yards long comprising 946 yards of single track and 700 yards of double track along Manchester Road, High Street, Market Street and Milnrow Road terminating near Small Brook road. There were seven passing loops varying in length from 77 to 165 yards.

2. A double track 1 mile 191 yards long commencing in Beal Lane, 108 yards from the level crossing, along Beal Lane and Rochdale Road terminating opposite the Old Bull's Head Inn.

2a. A double curve 18 yards long connecting Rochdale Road and Market Street.

2b. A double curve 18 yards long connecting Beal Lane and Market Street.

3. A continuation of tramway No. 2 of the Royton Order, 950 yards long comprising 218 yards single and 732 yards of double track along Oldham Road terminating by a junction with tramway No. 1 in High Street. There were three double track sections, 121, 480 and 132 yards in length.

On 24th October 1901, deputations from Royton and Crompton told Oldham that Provisional Orders for tramways had been obtained and that they were prepared to negotiate terms with Oldham to operate them. Oldham undertook to give the matter favourable consideration. Subsequently, Oldham intimated that it did not wish to lease tramway No. 2 of the Crompton Order.

After the opening of the route from Werneth Fire Station to the Royton boundary on 19th November

1902, the standard gauge steam trams had continued to operate from this point to Dogford Road, with narrow gauge traction from that point northwards. These services last ran on 30th May 1904. Although the lines in Royton had been authorised by the 1901 Order, a further Order was necessary in 1904 amending the remedies available to the Post Office in the event of damage to the telephone wires. A similar Order was also made in 1904 in respect of the lines authorised in Crompton. It had also been necessary for both authorities to apply to the Board of Trade in 1903 for an extension of time for the constructions of the tramways, action with which Oldham agreed.

Discussions had been taking place with both Royton and Crompton over Oldham's lease of the tramways which it was suggested should be on a similar basis to that of the Lees tramway. There was a problem with Royton which wanted the terms of the lease to recompense Royton for its portion of the purchase price of the steam company's undertaking.

The local authorities concerned – Royton, Rochdale and Bury – had valued the steam tramway undertaking at £123,784 (£5.8m) whereas the company was claiming £205,400 (£9.6m). Because of the failure of the parties to agree, the matter had gone to arbitration and the amount had not then been determined. Royton thought that the final award would be about £150,000 (£7.0m) and on the basis of two miles of route in Royton out of a total route mileage of 30 estimated the cost to Royton on a pro-rata basis at £10,000 (£470,000).

The basic financial principle of the lease was that Oldham would pay a rental which over 21 years would recover the capital cost and interest involved. Oldham offered to include in the capital cost a contribution towards the cost – not exceeding £10,000 – of the acquisition of the steam tramway in Royton less the amount realised from the sale of surplus company assets. During the course of the negotiations Royton belatedly realised that there were 2⅝ miles of route in Royton and not two as previously thought, and so suggested that the calculations should be based on £13,125 (£610,000) and not £10,000. Eventually, Royton offered Oldham three alternatives – two-thirds of the net cost based on £10,000 gross, half of the net cost based on the actual gross cost, or a sum of £5,000 (£235,000); Oldham opted for the last alternative. A further problem arose in January 1904 when the draft lease from Oldham excluded the Shaw Road line (tramway No. 1). Oldham then agreed to include it provided construction did not commence before 1st August 1906. The lease terms were eventually agreed on 5th April 1904.

In June Royton and Crompton appointed William Underwood and Brother of Dukinfield, Cheshire, to construct the line from the Royton boundary with Oldham to its boundary with Rochdale and the line from Higginshaw through Royton and Crompton to Shaw (Wren's Nest) at a tender price of £41,000 (£1.9m). W. T. Glover & Company Limited were appointed contractors for cabling and the Brush Electrical Engineering Company Limited undertook the overhead construction. Underwood commenced work on Tuesday, 19th July. It had been agreed in April to charge Royton and Crompton the cost price for materials supplied by Oldham.

Whilst construction of the Royton and Crompton lines was under way, Wilkinson resigned on being appointed general manager of Huddersfield Corporation Tramways. The Committee met on 26th September and appointed as successor Lewis Slattery out of 41 applicants, at a salary of £300 (£14,000) a year. At that time Slattery was the general manager of the Blackpool St. Annes & Lytham Tramway Company Limited.

Trial trips took place on 31st October 1904, on the first section completed followed by inspection next day by W. Trotter and Druitt – now promoted to Lieutenant-Colonel. The stretch comprised the reconstructed line in Royton from the boundary with Oldham to the boundary with Rochdale, a point known as Summit by Oldham and as Thornham by Rochdale (the latter had a Summit destination on its system beyond Littleborough). This tramway comprised a reconstruction of the 4 foot 8½ gauge steam tramway section from the Oldham-Royton boundary connecting with tramway No. 3 authorised by the 1901 Royton Order replacing the former 3 feet 6 inches gauge section of steam tramway in Royton to the Royton-Rochdale boundary. The new lines were single track with passing loops and as inspected totalled 2 miles 258 yards length overall of which 1 mile 690 yards was single line. The speed limits applied were 8 miles an hour in Oldham Road and 12 miles an hour in Rochdale Road. The section was opened to the public the same day (not 5th as stated in the Annual Reports). The Hathershaw – Royton boundary service via Rochdale Road was extended to Summit at a through fare of 3*d.* (59p). Rochdale had opened an electric tram service to the boundary with Royton on 5th October. The directors of the B.R.O. Company called an extraordinary general meeting for 10th November at which members voted for a voluntary winding-up.

Druitt inspected the line in Royton and Crompton from the Oldham boundary at Higginshaw to the outer terminus at Shaw (Wren's Nest) on 9th November. This extension represented tramway No. 2 of the Royton Order, tramway No. 3, and part of tramway No. 1, of the Crompton Order; the portion of tramway No. 1 not at that time constructed (Manchester Road) totalled 424 yards. Druitt recorded that all the lines were laid as described in the Orders with the lengths given therein. He also noted that some trees needed cutting in Higginshaw Lane and Heyside. The speed limits were generally 8 and 6 miles an hour; although the trees were dealt with by 30th November there were problems with the frontage to the Friends Meeting House in Heyside, near Turf Lane, where, it was claimed, the statutory frontager's notice had not been served. However, it was established that of 244 frontagers' notices served only one objected. Because of these matters the Board of Trade Certificate for the Royton portion was not issued until 27th January 1905; the Crompton Certificate was dated 24th November 1904. The service between Chadderton Road and Higginshaw was extended to Shaw (Wren's Nest) on the evening of the 17th at the through fare of 3*d.* for a distance of 4 miles 1,051 yards.

On 12th January 1905, a deputation representing Royton and Crompton urged Oldham to agree the immediate construction of the Shaw Road route to Shaw which Oldham had previously insisted should be deferred until August 1906. The contractor said that this would cost 5% less (approximately £500) if done immediately than if deferred. Oldham agreed provided the line was completed by 1st May 1905, and that as far as possible, material held in stock by Oldham was used in its construction. Work commenced on 9th February and the completed line was ready for inspection on 13th April, again by Druitt.

The party started from the Mumps depot at 11.30 a.m., travelling over the new line and then returning. It was constructed as single track with passing loops and comprised tramway No. 1 of the Royton Order and the remainder of tramway No. 1 of the Crompton Order. The former was 1 mile 97 yards including 1,510 yards of single track whilst the latter was 424 yards in length, single track apart from the extremities. A limit of 12 miles an hour was permitted in Shaw Road, Royton and Manchester Road, Crompton, with 4 miles an hour on various curves. It opened to the public the same day with a service between Shaw, Beal Lane (known also as Four Lane Ends) and Werneth fire station for a through fare of 3*d.*, thus extending the existing service between Royton and Werneth fire station.

The cost of the Royton and Crompton tramways was £61,583. 10*s.* 2*d.* (£2.9m) comprising £44,643. 14*s.* 4*d.* (£2.1m) for Royton and £16,939. 15*s.* 10*d.* (£0.8m) for Crompton. Under the terms of the lease agreement the capital cost for rental purposes was eventually agreed – in April 1911 – at £52,000 (£2.2m) for Royton and £18,350 (£0.8m) for Crompton. The Inland Revenue declined to refund tax deducted from the portion of the rent which represented capital repayment. The rents were £3,677. 11*s.* 8*d.* (£160,000) and £129. 17*s.* 10*d.* (£55,000) annually for Royton and Crompton respectively, the leases expiring on 31st December 1925.

In the following two years problems were encountered because, contrary to the specification, the trolley wires in Royton and Crompton had been installed at a different height from those in Oldham. Oldham told Royton and Crompton that they should insist on Brush adjusting the wires to conform with the Oldham height or, alternatively, pay £250 to cover Oldham's costs in doing so. After a certain amount of haggling, a payment of £100 (£4,300) by Brush was agreed in April 1907.

County Borough of Oldham.

Gourlay.  Mayor.

Inauguration of the Through Service of Cars between Oldham and Manchester.

Monday, January 21st, 1907.

Tramways Committee.

Mr. Councillor J. S. Dronsfield, J.P., Chairman.
Mr. Alderman S. Dunkerley, J.P., Vice-chairman.
The Mayor.
Mr. Councillor J. Greaves.
Mr. Councillor J. Heywood.
Mr. Councillor F. G. Isherwood, J.P.
Mr. Councillor J. Middleton.
Mr. Councillor T. Rothwell, J.P.
Mr. Councillor T. Smart.

J. H. Hallsworth, Town Clerk.
Lewis Slattery, General Manager.

Plate 32. For the Coronation of King George V and Queen Mary on 22nd June 1911, one of the open top trams was elaborately decorated with shields, bunting, evergreen and coloured lights. This tram toured the system, but a late night vigil would have been required to see the lights to the greatest effect.

Photo, McQuee

Plate 33. At the time of the Coronation, Oldham was taking delivery of its first twelve purpose built, balcony cars and one of these, believed to be No. 89, is seen here decorated in a much less elaborate fashion. It was known for some time subsequently as "The King George" tram. In the background can be seen No. 4, one of the original sample vehicles.

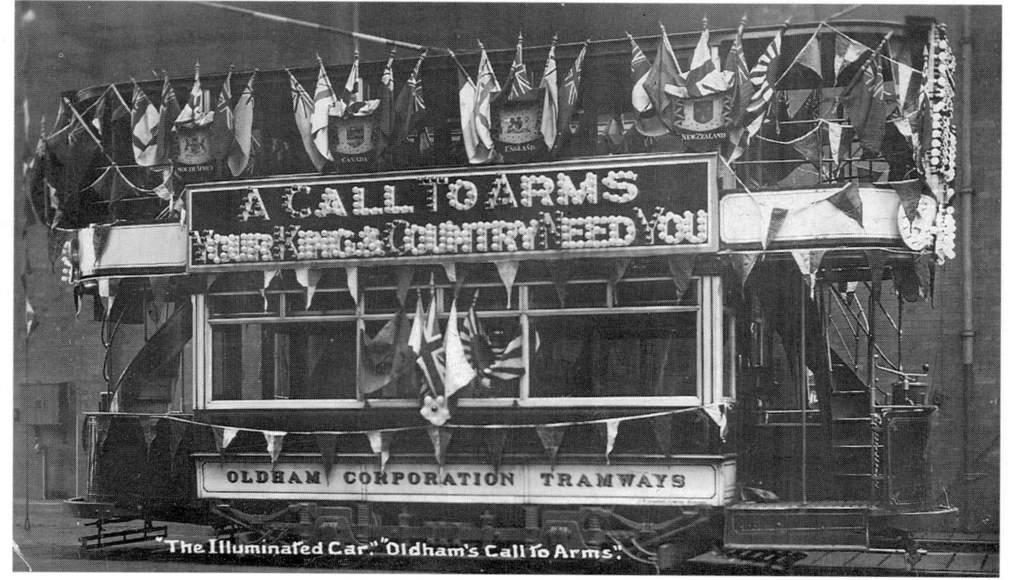

Plate 34. A visit by the King and Queen on 12th July 1913 was also marked by the preparation of a lavishly decorated open top tram. Regrettably the next decorated tram represented a less happy occasion, namely to serve as a recruiting car for World War I which had started on 4th August 1914. This car toured the system in October.

MUNICIPAL TRAMWAYS ASSOCIATION

MR. Slattery and John Heywood, a member of the Tramways Committee, attended the fourth annual conference of the Municipal Tramways Association held at the Agricultural Hall, London, during the Tramways and Light Railways exhibition in July 1905. The main points which emerged were the cost of electricity charged to Oldham tramways which was regarded as excessive, and the state of development of motor buses.

The delegates were unable to obtain any reliable data from the manufacturers since none of the buses on display had been running long enough to form a fair basis for working expenses and depreciation. The total working expenses of buses in Hastings were given as 10½*d.* per bus mile including 20% for depreciation. However, the Oldham representatives were dubious over these figures since they were given by the manufacturers, and considered that maintenance would increase year by year. The conclusion was "it does not appear that we have a severe competitor in the motor omnibus". They did note, however, that good progress had been made during the previous year, although they did not think they would stop the development of electric traction "we consider they will prove a valuable adjunct to tramways in acting as a feeder to existing lines by serving outlying districts that are sparsely populated".

Oldham was also impressed by an automatic point changer developed by a Leeds firm and subsequently had one fitted in King Street at the junction with Union Street. Rail joint welding also impressed them and they suggested a visit to Manchester where the process was in use.

An accident – which fortunately was not serious because the drivers remained at the controls – occurred on Middleton Road on the evening of Wednesday, 8th November 1905. Car 59 was moving slowly downhill in the lengthy stretch of double track extending from St. Domingo Street, and car 48 was travelling towards it on the single track section. Car 59 began to accelerate, so the driver of 48 stopped and then reversed, thus lessening the eventual impact of the other car which nevertheless was rather violent. Car 59 got out of control because the driver had not placed the slipper brake handle in position. As a result Mr. Slattery had an additional operating handle fitted to each tram so that if necessary, the conductor could apply the slipper brake from the rear platform.

Plate 35. On a happier note, Britannia was an adaptation of a tram to mark – on 19th July 1919 – the peace celebrations following the armistice on 11th November 1918. Britannia is seen here in Hollinwood depot with open top tram No. 40 alongside. Oldham invited servicemen and children of those who had lost their lives to inspect this vehicle on 26th July.

Plate 36. A general scene in Huddersfield Road in which a Manchester balcony car can just be glimpsed beyond the Oldham vehicle. *Photo, Chas Wilkinson*

Plate 37. Middleton Road, Chadderton, in the traction company era. The distinctive style of the scroll work is clearly evident. *Photo, Gudger*

THROUGH RUNNING TO ROCHDALE AND MANCHESTER

THE next major development was the introduction of joint through running over adjacent systems. The first of these was with Rochdale, when cars of both authorities provided a through route between Hathershaw and Norden which point was 2 miles 1,329 yards north west of Rochdale town centre on the road to Accrington; this commenced on 1st May 1906, and was confirmed after the original 12 months' trial period.

The question of through running between Manchester and Oldham had first been raised at a meeting between the two authorities in February 1903 when Manchester asked for running powers to Waterhead. The matter lay dormant until July 1905 when Oldham asked whether Manchester was now prepared to discuss the subject further. The outcome was that in October, a deputation from Oldham suggested that a through service should be established between Piccadilly and Waterhead, each corporation providing and running its proper proportion of the rolling stock, the whole of the earnings in each authority's area to be handed over to that authority. Heads of agreement were established by the two undertakings by May 1906 under which the cars and crews would be provided by each party pro rata to route mileage, any excess mileage to be paid for at an agreed figure. No advertisements were to be permitted on the cars, which were to be as nearly as possible of equal seating capacity. The gross earnings in each corporation's area were to be paid over to that corporation entailing separate tickets to be provided by each operator for use in its own district. The cost of connecting the tracks at Hollinwood (the Oldham / Failsworth boundary) was to be borne equally by the two authorities.

At that time, Manchester was operating large (bogie) cars on the service to Hollinwood and under the proposals small cars would have to be adopted to give near equality of seating capacity with Oldham. It was also necessary to equip the Manchester cars with slipper brakes because of the gradients in Oldham. An order was placed for these in October, and Manchester hoped to start the service on 1st January 1907.

Manchester took the view that it had powers to enter into the agreement for through running without the agreement of Failsworth whose lines were leased to Manchester, but nevertheless thought it desirable to tell Failsworth before entering into an agreement. Manchester therefore informed Failsworth of the intentions of the two authorities, at the same time setting out the basis on which it claimed to have the powers to do so.

This prompted a visit from Failsworth objecting to the proposed through running and indicating that the council would require some consideration by way of payment of an increased rental. Failsworth also suggested running an additional workmen's car from Failsworth at 6 a.m., the running of additional workmen's cars in the evenings between Failsworth and Piccadilly; 1½*d.* workmen's fare between Failsworth and Piccadilly; the name Failsworth to be displayed on the cars; Manchester to water the roadway in the district, and particulars of the proposed through service to be furnished to the district council.

Manchester conceded the 1½*d.* workmen's fare and the extra car in the morning but deferred the proposal regarding evening cars to await the outcome of a general enquiry on the topic. Failsworth was to be displayed on the route boards and cars would continue to be run between Hollinwood and Piccadilly. Manchester could not undertake the watering of the roadway. On 12th July, the clerk to the Failsworth council wrote to Manchester as follows:

The council "...contend that the lease to your Corporation never contemplated the use of their tramways by the Oldham Corporation otherwise apt words to that effect would have been inserted in it. Moreover, the lease is a lease of the tramways as they were laid down at the time from which the lease runs, namely, 1st April 1903, and as then laid down the tramlines did not extend to the lines of the Oldham Corporation, and therefore there could not be any running over the Oldham lines by Manchester or running over the Failsworth lines by Oldham. The general provisions of the lease show clearly that Manchester only has the right to use the Failsworth lines. It is true that section 6 of the Manchester Corporation Tramways Act, 1899, empowers that Corporation to arrange with Oldham and other towns for running over each others lines, but it does not nor does the lease authorise this to be done without the sanction of the owners of the tramlines which are not within their own respective districts.

"I am further directed to call the attention of your Corporation to the fact that they have recently, in a surreptitious manner, extended the Failsworth tramlines so as to join the Oldham lines. This has been done without the knowledge or consent of the District Council and amounts to a trespass on the roadway, and they would be glad to know under what authority your Corporation presumed to do this work. Unless some authority can be shown to exist, the District Council will remove the lines that have been laid down.

"Having regard to the strong views which the District Council entertain on the subject of this letter, they hope that your Corporation will not take any further steps in the matter without their sanction. The lease provides that any dispute or difference shall be referred to the Board of Trade"

After further discussion Failsworth, whilst reiterating its previous view about the legality of the situation, decided not to press its case any further provided satisfactory arrangements were made for running workmen's cars in the evenings and for preventing the through traffic from interfering unduly with local traffic to and from Failsworth.

It was not until 21st January 1907, that the through running started. The event was handsomely celebrated. The Manchester Tramways Committee and other members of the City Council together with the Lord Mayor assembled at the Manchester Town Hall at 2.30 p.m. and left for Oldham 15 minutes later in five special trams. The first of these was an open top bogie car decorated with 1,800 electric lights of various colours and garlanded with green leaves, accompanied by four open top single truck cars, festooned with artificial green leaves on the sides and bedecked with miniature flags.

The procession travelled to Hollinwood where several Oldham cars were drawn up on the other track. At this point, a ribbon had been stretched across the road and the Lord Mayor, having been presented with a pair of silver scissors, leaned forward from the platform of the first tram and cut the tape. This ceremony was marked by short speeches, the Chairman of the Manchester Tramways Committee commenting that in cutting the tape, the Lord Major had cut away the obstructions, while the Mayor of Oldham, Dr. Robert Gourlay, referred to it as an emblem of the goodwill and harmony that existed between the two authorities.

The Lord Mayor drove for a short distance and the Oldham cars followed on behind the Manchester vehicles. Despite the fact that the mills were at work, large crowds thronged the route to cheer the procession on. "Dense crowds" had assembled at the Town Hall, where the Oldham police band greeted the convoy with "See The Conquering Hero Comes".

The civic leaders again exchanged compliments and the convoy then travelled on to Waterhead returning to the Town Hall where about 150 guests had "a knife-and-fork tea". Here again, the event was fittingly celebrated, Councillor Middleton proposed a toast to the Lord Mayor and citizens of Manchester and claimed that tramways, like railways, might be said to be the agents of civilisation, although there was nothing to civilise in Oldham where people spoke plain English with a local accent.

During the festivities in the Town Hall, the illuminated car returned to Manchester and then journeyed back to Oldham again, leaving Piccadilly at 6.00 p.m., with the Lady Mayoress and other female guests; by this time the lights had been switched on to the great approval and delight of the multitudes of spectators.

The procession once again travelled to Waterhead and then made its way to Manchester with the Oldham cars leading, and the "gorgeous brilliance" of the display was admired by thousands on the way to Manchester.

At the Failsworth boundary, the ceremony performed on the outward journey was repeated, with the Mayor of Oldham this time playing the major role. The police band was still in evidence and the departure was made to the strains of "We Won't Go Home Till Morning". Thus ended the great occasion.

The through route was nearly 9 miles long and the journey took 65 minutes at a total cost of 6*d.* which comprised 3*d.* for the journey in each authority's area; from Oldham Market Place to Manchester the fare was 5*d.* (96p). Seven Manchester and six Oldham cars provided a 10 minute service from 6.55 a.m. to 11.05 p.m. The fare for the Manchester portion was reduced to 2½*d.* in October, 1909, and to 2*d.* (35p) in 1913.

The inauguration of the through services prompted a request from Lees in March for a similar facility but this was turned down by Oldham. It was soon found that the cars from both Oldham and Manchester reversing at Hollinwood were delaying the through service and accordingly two extra tracks were laid to facilitate their passage, the inner tracks being used for cars reversing. Possibly as a result of Oldham's experience in St. Domingo Street, the 9 foot 6 inch margin between kerb and

Plate 38. Fleet No. 5 of the Middleton Electric Traction Company seen at the single-track terminus at the boundary of Chadderton and Oldham near the Free Trade Inn. Although the Oldham trams terminated a few yards beyond this point, the general lack of connections, as on this occasion, gave rise to much complaint.

Plate 39. Oldham tram 44 at the boundary with Chadderton and on this occasion there is no traction company tram in evidence. The Oldham terminal point had a double track hence the position of the tram to one side of the road. The Free Trade Inn is clearly in evidence in the left foreground.
Photo, Allen & Sons

nearside rails was achieved by reducing the space between the original tracks. The new arrangements came into force on 14th October 1908. The cost was £1056. 9*s.* 1*d.* (£47,000), shared equally with Manchester. In December 1908, Shaw wanted a through service to Manchester but Oldham countered the request by saying that it was short of trams and also that it had no agreement with Manchester.

In 1909 Oldham was investigating the possibility of introducing more top covered cars on the route; Manchester continued to operate open-top cars, influenced it is thought by the gradients in Oldham. However, on 25th January 1910, the Oldham Committee travelled to Hollinwood where they met the Manchester Committee who had travelled from Manchester in "the first top covered car for the through route". The party inspected the new depot (mentioned later) and then travelled on the Manchester car to Waterhead. On the return journey they inspected the Wallshaw depot and two cars which were being fitted with top covers. The Manchester car would have been a four wheel balcony type.

Although the through service originally operated to Piccadilly in Manchester it was curtailed to a new terminal in Stevenson Square about 200 yards short of Piccadilly on 4th August 1910; the new terminal was also used from the same date by three other services and by short workings and was introduced in order to reduce obstruction in Piccadilly to cars on routes passing through the city centre.

PROPOSED TRAMWAYS IN SADDLEWORTH AND SPRINGHEAD

IT is now necessary to retrace our steps to October 1899 when Oldham received a letter from the United Kingdom Tramway Light Railway and Electrical Syndicate Limited, asking for a deputation to be received regarding proposed tramways in the Saddleworth district running into Oldham. The matter was dealt with by informing the company that Oldham would oppose any action by the company which might affect Oldham; it was also decided to oppose any company seeking to lay lines in Oldham. The matter then seems to have lain dormant until July 1901, when Lees was told, regarding proposals in Saddleworth and Springhead, that Oldham could not entertain running over Oldham tracks. A deputation from Springhead Urban District in October also had no success. In November, a Bill seeking powers for a company to operate tramways in Saddleworth, Springhead and Lees, and to run over Oldham tracks by agreement, was published. Not surprisingly, Oldham opposed it. Proposed tramways six and eight related to lines in Lees and the Parish of Cross Bank and, given Oldham's attitude and Lees' desire for through running to Oldham, were struck out during the parliamentary process.

The outcome of the Bill was that the Saddleworth and Springhead Tramways Company was authorised by the Saddleworth and Springhead Tramways Act, 1902, to construct tramways in the Urban Districts of Saddleworth and Springhead in the West Riding of Yorkshire and in the Rural District of Limehurst in Lancashire totalling 13 miles 604 yards of route. Tramway No. 4 commenced at the Waterhead terminus in Huddersfield Road; tramway No. 5 ran from the termination of tramway No. 1 (not then constructed) authorised by the contemporary 1902 Lees Order at the boundary of Lees and Springhead.

The over-ambitious nature of the project was recognised in the Saddleworth and Springhead Tramways Act, 1904 which authorised the abandonment of tramways Nos. 3 and 4 representing 5 miles 1021 yards and also conferred a reduction in the share capital of the company from £150,000 (£7.0m) to £135,000 (£6.3m), with a sharp reduction in the borrowing powers. Additionally, the Act authorised a part refund of the deposit money to the extent that it represented that portion of the cost of the scheme relating to tramways Nos. 3 and 4 and also to the proposed tramways Nos. 6 and 8 given that they were struck out of the original Bill. Lastly, the name of the company was changed to the Oldham and Saddleworth District Tramways Company.

The company found it expedient to be authorised to raise additional capital and to be granted further powers, which were duly conferred by the Oldham and Saddleworth District Tramways Act 1905. This Act authorised a tramroad which was part tramway, 1399 yards long comprising single and double track. It lay partly in the West Riding of Yorkshire and partly in Lancashire commencing at the boundary of Springhead with the Borough of Mossley in Under Lane near the junction of Butt Lane, by a junction with tramway No. 7 of the 1902 Act; it passed through private lands in Springhead and Mossley, then along Waterton Lane and Lancaster Street terminating by a junction with the existing tramway of the Stalybridge, Hyde, Mossley and Dukinfield Tramways and Electricity Board in Stamford Street, Mossley.

Over twelve months later there was no progress towards construction and efforts were made in January 1907 to interest Oldham to undertake the working of these tramways. The general manager had inspected the route of the proposed lines, and the Tramways Committee shared his view that the lines would not be profitable. Given the difficulties that Oldham itself had encountered in profitable operation of a much more compact urban system, it is surprising that as many as three Acts were put on the statute book for these relatively sparsely populated areas.

The scheme saw further press coverage in April 1908. Somewhat optimistically, the report said that if the plans went through it was expected that cars would be running over the new system before the August bank holiday! It was claimed that a prospectus would shortly be issued. The solicitor to the promoters was Sir W.H. Vaudrey, who had been Lord Mayor of Manchester in 1898-99; he had also been involved in the promotion of tramway schemes south of Manchester, through the Manchester Southern Tramways (Lancashire) and the Manchester Southern Tramways (Cheshire) Bills.

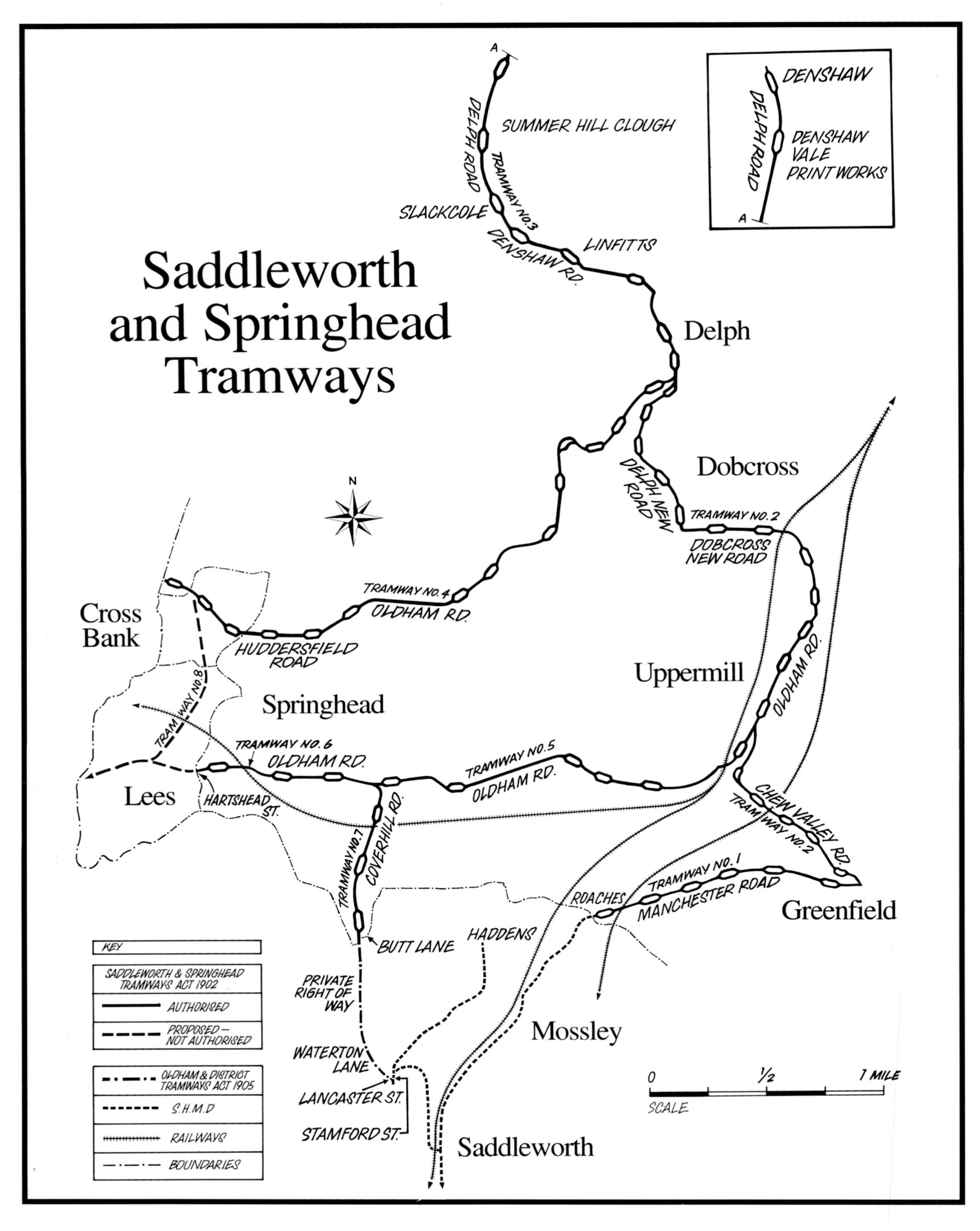
Saddleworth and Springhead Tramways
DENSHAW
DELPH ROAD
DENSHAW VALE PRINT WORKS
A
SUMMER HILL CLOUGH
DELPH ROAD
TRAMWAY NO.3
SLACKCOLE
DENSHAW RD.
LINFITTS
Delph
Dobcross
DELPH NEW ROAD
TRAMWAY NO.2
DOBCROSS NEW ROAD
N
Cross Bank
TRAMWAY NO.4
OLDHAM RD.
HUDDERSFIELD ROAD
Uppermill
OLDHAM RD.
Springhead
TRAMWAY NO.8
TRAMWAY NO.6
OLDHAM RD.
TRAMWAY NO.5
OLDHAM RD.
Lees
HARTSHEAD ST.
COVERHILL RD.
TRAMWAY NO.7
CHEW VALLEY RD.
TRAMWAY NO.2
TRAMWAY NO.1
MANCHESTER ROAD
ROACHES
Greenfield
BUTT LANE
HADDENS
PRIVATE RIGHT OF WAY
Mossley
WATERTON LANE
LANCASTER ST.
STAMFORD ST.
Saddleworth
0
½
1 MILE
SCALE
KEY
SADDLEWORTH & SPRINGHEAD TRAMWAYS ACT 1902
AUTHORISED
PROPOSED — NOT AUTHORISED
OLDHAM & DISTRICT TRAMWAYS ACT 1905
S.H.M.D
RAILWAYS
BOUNDARIES

PROFIT OR LOSS?

IN his annual report for the year to March 1907 Mr. Slattery drew attention to the depreciation policy being pursued. He pointed out that the period allowed by the Acts for the redemption of loans for track construction was 30 years whereas the life of the track in his view would not exceed 15 years. It followed therefore that provision should be made to relay the track after the shorter period by providing additional sums yearly which with the existing contribution to the sinking fund would cover the cost of such work. He warned the committee that if such a policy were not followed it would be necessary to provide either out of revenue or the rates the shortfall of the sinking fund in relation to the reconstruction costs. He also reminded the committee that Oldham could only reborrow to the extent to which provision had been made for the redemption of the original loan debt. In its 1899 Act Oldham was empowered to provide out of revenue a reserve fund by setting aside such sums as were considered reasonable, for investment in approved securities.

Mr. Slattery returned to the subject in his next annual report and informed the committee that "I deeply deplore your decision to hand over the sum of £3,000 in relief of the rates out of this year's surplus, which must not be considered profit in the true meaning of the word." He reiterated that compared with the financial provision based on a life of 30 years, "it is now generally agreed that the estimated life of tramway track bearing 50,000 car miles per annum is approximately 14 to 15 years". He therefore asked the Committee to "consider the matter from a financial point of view before contributing towards the relief of the rates in future years".

When the accounts for the year to March 1909 showed a return to deficit he again asked for serious consideration of the financial implications of track repairs.

"The fact that there has been a deficiency during the past year should not, in my opinion, deter the Committee from proceeding with this work, even if the cost thereof has to be borne out of the rates. I have again to remind you that the contributions to the sinking fund provide for renewal of the track at the end of 30 years, whereas it is universally accepted by the various technical institutions, and agreed by the Income Tax authorities, that the life of a tramway track bearing 50,000 car miles per annum does not exceed fourteen years. It is, therefore, obvious that some further provision in addition to the sinking fund contribution should be seriously considered."

A continuing theme of Mr. Slattery's tenure of office was that the department was paying an exorbitant price for electricity. He returned to the subject in November 1908 with a special report. Figures showed that for 11 operators within a 30 mile radius of Oldham supplied by a power station providing electricity for both lighting and traction, the price paid per Board of Trade unit varied from 1·0*d.* in Bury to 1·5*d.* (28p) at Oldham whose load factor of 27% was the highest of the undertakings covered apart from Manchester which was 32·7%. Manchester was in fact paying 1·143*d.* (21p) a unit for an annual consumption of 30 million units compared with Oldham's 3,888,404 units. The smallest consumption was at Ashton where 1·25*d.* per unit was paid for 622,913 units. In five instances – Burnley, Halifax, Manchester, Salford and Stockport, cabling had been supplied by and maintained by the electricity department. In the case of Oldham and the others in the survey this expense was borne by the tramways department.

Mr. Slattery thought that Oldham was as well situated as the other users for coal supplies, an important factor in the works cost of generation. He thought that the works cost at Oldham compared very favourably with most towns and that therefore the electricity department was being maintained by and at the expense of the tramways department. For eleven operators throughout the country which had their own power station, total costs of generation, including establishment charges, ranged from 0·62*d.* (11p) to 1·191*d.* (22p) apart from Bournemouth which, exceptionally, was 1·626*d.* (30p) reflecting its remoteness from the coalfields. Mr. Slattery's conclusion was that the electricity could be profitably supplied at 1*d.* a unit which, on the consumption in the year to March 1908, would have resulted in an additional surplus for the tramways of £8,100. 16*s.* 10*d.* (£360,000).

He believed that private customers were supplied with current for power purposes between certain hours at 1*d.* a unit metered at their own works without regard to any charge for the cost of laying the main feeders, maintaining them, or for transmission losses. Although the price of current for lighting and power purposes had recently been reduced to private customers, the tramways had not benefited notwithstanding that its consumption had almost doubled over the past five years and that it was the largest customer. His final comment was that "this department own and maintain all feeders from the switchboard at the generating station; suffer all transmission losses from that point, and notwithstanding our enormous consumption are called upon to pay 1½*d.* a unit.

Plate 40. The junction of Union Street and Yorkshire Street. *Photo, J. L. Brown*

Plate 41. The built-up nature of the town's tram routes is well illustrated in this picture of Ashton Road. *Photo, Allen & Sons*

OLDHAM CORPORATION ACT 1909

IN 1908 Oldham was considering the promotion of a general Bill for the execution of various works including additional tramways. In July, the Tramways Committee suggested powers for lines in Napier Street East, Coppice Street, Chamber Road and Gainsborough Road to Copster Hill but these did not materialise. Following opposition, powers for trolleybuses were deleted from the proposed Bill.

A deputation from Chadderton in August requested an extension to Eaves Lane. Chadderton was informed in February 1909 that Oldham would operate tramways in Chadderton, including the Middleton Electric Traction Company's line, if satisfactory terms could be agreed.

Under the Oldham Corporation Act 1909, Oldham, was enabled to enter into through running arrangements with other operators, including companies; powers for operating buses within Oldham were also granted. The following tramways were authorised:

1. A line 363 yards long comprising 154 yards single and 209 yards of double track commencing in King Street by a junction with the existing tramway (No. 1 of the 1882 Order) across Union Street and along George Street terminating in the Market Place by a junction with the existing tramway (No. 1 of the 1878 Order).

1a. A line 32 yards long comprising 12 yards single and 20 yards of double track connecting tramway No. 1 in George Street in a north-westerly direction to the Market Place tramway.

2. A line 279 yards long comprising 119 yards single and 160 yards of double track commencing in Middleton Road by a junction with the existing tramway (No. 3 of the 1899 Act) along West Street terminating in Market Place by a junction with the existing tramway.

3. A line 1,674 yards long comprising 1,102 yards single and 572 yards of double track in Ripponden Road, representing an extension of the existing tramway (No. 9 of the 1899 Act) to the borough boundary.

4. A line 612 yards long comprising 325 yards single and 287 yards of double track along Oxford Street from a junction with the existing tramway in Manchester Road (No. 1 of the 1878 Order) to the Chadderton boundary at Block Lane.

Oldham Corporation Tramways.

Formal Opening of the Tramways,

Monday, 19th May, 1902.

H. C. LEE & CO., KING ST., OLDHAM.

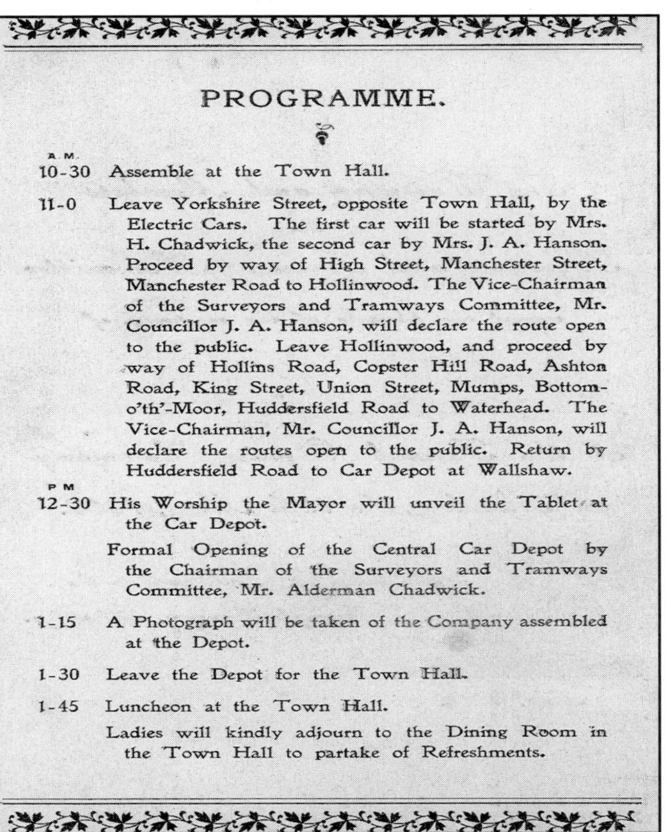

PROGRAMME.

A.M.
10-30 Assemble at the Town Hall.

11-0 Leave Yorkshire Street, opposite Town Hall, by the Electric Cars. The first car will be started by Mrs. H. Chadwick, the second car by Mrs. J. A. Hanson. Proceed by way of High Street, Manchester Street, Manchester Road to Hollinwood. The Vice-Chairman of the Surveyors and Tramways Committee, Mr. Councillor J. A. Hanson, will declare the route open to the public. Leave Hollinwood, and proceed by way of Hollins Road, Copster Hill Road, Ashton Road, King Street, Union Street, Mumps, Bottom-o'th'-Moor, Huddersfield Road to Waterhead. The Vice-Chairman, Mr. Councillor J. A. Hanson, will declare the routes open to the public. Return by Huddersfield Road to Car Depot at Wallshaw.

P.M.
12-30 His Worship the Mayor will unveil the Tablet at the Car Depot.

Formal Opening of the Central Car Depot by the Chairman of the Surveyors and Tramways Committee, Mr. Alderman Chadwick.

1-15 A Photograph will be taken of the Company assembled at the Depot.

1-30 Leave the Depot for the Town Hall.

1-45 Luncheon at the Town Hall.

Ladies will kindly adjourn to the Dining Room in the Town Hall to partake of Refreshments.

Courtesy Oldham Local Studies Library.

HOLLINWOOD DEPOT

A YEAR after the opening of the through route to Manchester, Oldham had to turn its attention to increasing the depot accommodation to cope with the increasing maintenance and expansion of the tram car fleet. The small temporary depot in Neville Street stood on part of a larger site which had originally been earmarked for a major depot scheme. However, on 2nd January 1908, after due consideration and visiting the site, the Committee decided to acquire a plot of land at Hollinwood just on the Oldham side of the border with Failsworth. The site was close to Stable Street, the location of the Carriage Company's former horse tram depot which served the Oldham routes. Plans were drawn up and construction duly commenced. The official opening took place on 18th August 1910, by the Major, Alderman Schofield. The whole site area was 4,180 square yards. The various buildings included the main running shed measuring 240 x 70 feet which could accommodate 40 trams; the paint shop could hold three or four. Alderman Dunkerley unveiled a marble tablet commemorating the opening. On the following Saturday and Sunday the depot was open for inspection by the public between 2.00 p.m. and 6.00 p.m. with the manager and officials in attendance. The following January Oldham accepted an offer for the Neville Street land and another - of £10 (£430) - for the wooden car shed, but specifically excluding the rails.

Plate 42. Car 94 seen in King Street having just crossed Union Street. The point boy can be seen looking into his hut on the left.

Photo, Charles Wilkinson courtesy E. Gray

Plate 43. The Summit terminus of route No. 7 shown looking towards Oldham in the mid 20s.

Photo, Fieldings Series courtesy A. Lindley

MORE CONSTRUCTION

On 2nd August, 1909, the service between Union Street West and Mumps Bridge was extended from the Bridge to Waterhead; the new arrangement had not been going long before on 25th October it was supplemented by the reinstatement of the original shorter service.

A serious accident happened at 5.30 a.m. on Friday, 10th June 1910, when two trams met head on on a single track section near the Railway Hotel in East Crompton. Open-top No. 38, with about 30 passengers, had left Werneth at 5.0 a.m. for Wren's Nest, Shaw, whilst the other, covered-top car No. 47, had left Wren's Nest at 5.24 a.m. for Chadderton Road with two or three passengers. Several people were injured, many of them operatives at the Hawk Mill which as a result was short of workers. The open-top car was badly damaged, needing a new platform amongst other items, but the scene was cleared by 7.00 a.m.

On 11th April 1910, the Committee inspected Watersheddings Street and Sheepfoot Lane as possible sites for sidings for traffic to the rugby league football ground and Oldham Athletic football ground respectively but eventually decided in August to approach the frontagers for a planned siding in Broadbent Road. Nothing came of this proposal.

Early in 1910, it was decided to lay the tracks in George Street (tramways Nos. 1 and 1A of the 1909 Act) using Edmondson and Wyatt of Dover Street, Werneth, as contractors. The rails were Thermit welded, and the overhead was erected by the department. Track construction cost £2,661. 14*s.* 9*d.* (£120,000) and the overhead £290. 10*s.* 5*d.* (£13,000). Both these lines, totalling 395 yards, were inspected by Druitt on 2nd December 1910. He also inspected a short length of line in Crossbank Street, 235 yards long of which 175 yards was single track, which represented the reconstruction of the former horse tramway in this Street, authorised by the 1878 Tramways Order. This was to provide an alternative route in case of any blockage on the direct route to Yorkshire Street.

Druitt reported that "the permanent way and overhead equipment had been very well constructed" and fixed speed limits of 10 miles an hour in each street. Oldham brought the George Street tracks into use on the 5th by diverting the Moorside and Hollinwood route from Union Street to Yorkshire Street and George Street. George Street was constructed as specified in the Act.

Later in the month, Slattery resigned on being appointed assistant to the Chief Officer of the tramways department of London County Council. He was succeeded the following month by Joseph W. Dugdale, General Manager and Engineer of Ashton-under-Lyne Corporation Tramways, selected from 92 applicants, at a salary of £350 (£15,400). Evidence of new thinking was apparent in May when it was agreed that in future the department would be responsible for all maintenance of the tracks and the tramway margins, including the lines leased in the adjacent urban districts.

On 9th June, a service was introduced from Union Street West via Union Street to Hill Stores on Ripponden Road; it lasted only a few weeks before being replaced on 24th July by a longer service – Union Street West to Watersheddings, and a shorter one – Union Street West to Mumps Bridge.

Plate 44. A view of Mumps showing on the left balcony car 34 and on the right number 40 shortly after its conversion to fully enclosed state in 1921. *Photo, Chas Wilkinson*

Plate 45. In the early post War years a car on route 5 to Grains Bar emerges from George Street into Market Place. The elaborate fountain to its right was removed to Alexandra Park early in 1923.

Photo, Chas Wilkinson

Plate 46. Another typical Oldham Street scene in Manchester Road at its junction with Cross Bank Street.

Photo, Allen & Sons

Plate 47. Car 54 standing at the Shaw terminus was rebuilt to this all enclosed condition in the early 1920s. The trolley has not been aversed but the destination has already been set for the journey to Chadderton Road.

Photo, A. J. Lees

Edmondson and Wyatt were appointed to construct the tramway in West Street (No. 2 of the 1909 Act) which was a continuation of the Middleton Road tramway. The work included a curve from St. Domingo Street, but not from Rochdale Road, which was the continuation across the Middleton Road - West Street intersection. A problem arose on this contract in December when the Town Clerk pointed out that, contrary to the specification requiring British rails, German material had been delivered to the site. The contractor explained that the rails had been ordered through Dick Kerr and through an oversight British material had not been specified. Urgent resolution of the problem was essential because the street had been taken up in order to lay the rails. Oldham was told that no British material was readily available and on the contractor's offer to give a discount, and assurance that the German material was not of inferior quality, Oldham acquiesced in the use of the German rails. Construction cost £1,526. 15*s.* 3*d.* (£64,000), special track work £501. 10*s.* 0*d.* (£21,000), and overhead equipment £274. 15*s.* 10*d.* (£11,000).

Druitt returned to Oldham on 19th April 1912 to inspect the line. The inspection party travelled in the morning over the new section to St. Domingo Street, and returned to the Mumps depot. Druitt imposed a six mile per hour speed limit and compulsory stops before crossing Grimshaw Street on the downward journey and in both directions before crossing Rochdale Road / St. Domingo Street. As constructed the line was 285 yards long of which 143 yards was double track. On 22nd April the Middleton Road cars commenced running to Market Place instead of Star Inn.

Plate 48. One of the cars delivered in 1919 passing through Failsworth on its journey from Manchester to Waterhead *Photo, Buckley*

Plate 49. Market Place showing the overhead tower wagon in operation. Their task is not as big as might appear since the overhead has been removed by the publisher of the postcard!

SOME ACCIDENTS

A HEAD-ON collision between a single-deck car bound for Shaw and a double-deck car travelling to Oldham took place on a piece of single track in Royton a few minutes before 6.00 a.m. on 11th April 1912. The double-deck car mounted on top of the fender of the single-deck car, the driver of which was pinned underneath the front of the double-decker.

The accident happened on the long single-track section north of the Oldham boundary at Longsight. In the past there had been many complaints about delays due to cars meeting on the single line resulting in one car having to turn back. As a result electric light signals had been installed at both ends of the section indicating to a driver whether the section was occupied. It would appear that one driver ignored the signal or didn't see it because it was foggy and because of the fog the drivers could not see from one loop to the next.

On 21st August 1912 Lees expressed concern to Oldham about the 'excessive speed' of some trams when descending from County End, and at Salem Brow, and the state of the road at Lees Brook. Oldham promised that the matters would be attended to.

Lee's worst fears were realised on Monday 23rd December, when an accident occurred shortly after 7.00 p.m. Tram No. 92 which at that time was the newest car in the fleet, was travelling to Lees on the down gradient at Salem Brow when, seemingly out of control, it passed through the loop at a very high speed and on the single track section collided head on with car No. 38 which had left Lees at 7.00 p.m. The force of the impact flung the driver of car 38 out on to the road and the tram started going backwards down the hill. The conductor closed the door at his end of the car to stop passengers attempting to get off, whilst applying the brake. Seeing the other car bearing down he then let it run further down through the Gibraltar Street loop which is where car 92 was eventually brought to a halt.

The magnetic brake of car 92 was found to be in perfect order and it was thought that initial application of the brake had led the car to slide on the greasy rails before further application of the brake brought it to a halt. In due course it was driven back to the depot under its own power. Car 38 was very badly damaged at the driver's end and after removal of various items of twisted metal it was towed back to the depot. There were about 12 female passengers in the saloon of 38 and about six males on top and fortunately none was injured. Car No. 93, a covered top balcony open vestibule car, made its appearance in the Oldham fleet in the next few months without any increase in the total fleet; it seems likely that this was in fact a rebuild of the damaged No. 38, which it will be recalled, had already been involved in a collision at Crompton in 1910, given that the water car was in due course numbered 38.

Plate 50. To the left of the photograph part of a Manchester balcony tram can be seen outside Ashton Town Hall with an SHMD vehicle nearer the camera; on the right there is an Oldham open-top tram on the 14 route waiting to depart for Star Inn.
Photo, Chas Wilkinson

REOPENING OF EGERTON STREET LINE

IT was mentioned earlier that the service from Higginshaw along Egerton Street, Radcliffe Street and Rock Street to Lord Street operated for the last time on 17th April 1904, after a life of a little over two years. In the years following, Oldham had purchased property at the corner of Rock Street and Radcliffe Street to enable the track at this point to be improved. On 7th December 1911, it was agreed that curves should be inserted at this point; these were inspected on 21st December when the satisfactory passage of a tram was also witnessed, and the route reopened again on this day, with a service from Shaw. Unfortunately, the receipts on this were most unsatisfactory at 4·92*d.* (85p) per car mile, compared with 12·95*d.* (£2.25) on the whole system, and at a meeting in August 1912 the Committee agreed to discontinue this service again, this time for good, from 14th September. In December it was decided to lift the diamond crossings in Cross Street, which was apparently no longer used.

Plate 51. After only four years operation the trams to Ashton were replaced by trolleybuses; here one of the Ashton vehicles is seen at Bardsley. *Photo, F. Brierley*

Plate 52. Over the tram route from Hathershaw to Star Inn the trolleybuses shared the positive wire with the tramways. The trolleybuses ran to the Star Inn only for about twelve months. *Photo, Lilywhite Ltd*

EXTENSION TO GRAINS BAR

WE now come to the long running saga of what proved to be Oldham's last new tramway construction. As early as October 1907 the Committee inspected the section of Ripponden Road from the then terminus at Moorside to the Oldham boundary at Grains Bar, as an extension requested by the residents. The cost was estimated at £10,000 (£450,000). At a meeting on 3rd August 1911 Dugdale reported on his recent visit to the newly inaugurated trolleybus systems (then known as trackless trams) at Bradford and Leeds.

He agreed the "motorbus principle" as feeders to the tramways for outlying districts and suggested that the "new system" should be used on the projected extension to Grains Bar. Thereby it was estimated that the cost would be some £1300 (£56,000) per mile instead of £13000 (£560,000) per mile. The interest generated was such that on 18th September the Committee also visited the Leeds and Bradford systems.

The outcome of the various discussions was that in December Oldham asked the Board of Trade if the authorised extension of the tramways to Grains Bar could be operated by trolleybuses without further sanction. Oldham pointed out that a tramway had been authorised, and Oldham had powers to operate buses in the borough, and suggested sending a deputation. However the idea of a deputation was quickly abandoned when the Board of Trade indicated that new powers would be required. In February 1912 it was decided to investigate what it would cost to construct the extension if the work was done by Oldham. However, three months later it was concluded that it would be "undesirable" to proceed with the extension at that time.

A year later, following the purchase of buses to operate in the Coppice Road area on weekdays, a bus service was provided on Saturdays and Sundays between Moorside and Grains Bar. However, residents presented a petition and sent a deputation in August 1913 complaining of the nuisance caused by the buses on this section. It was agreed to ask the borough surveyor what steps he was taking to improve the surface of Ripponden Road and also obtain an estimate for extending the trams from Moorside. The outcome was that in November it was at last agreed to go ahead with the extension (tramway No. 3 of the 1909 Act) and as far as possible to use material salvaged from the Egerton Street route which, as noted earlier, had closed in September 1912. In February 1914, it was reported that poles from Egerton Street and Cross Street were already on site and work on the extension started on the 23rd. Walter Scott Ltd. provided rails for this project.

An average of 110 people were employed and ten days were lost through rain; in addition it took eight days to deal with a large bog hole some 40 to 60 yards long which necessitated foundations of heavy boulders down to six feet. This was reinforced with old tram rails 30 feet long interlaced with smaller

Plate 53. An interesting scene in the middle 1920s showing a car on route 9 turning into Henshaw Street and, on the left, one of the Manchester freight trams. *Photo, J. L. Brown*

pieces, totalling up to ten tons, the foundation then being topped with two feet of concrete.

The Committee visited Grains Bar to review progress in March and again on 25th May when the work was almost complete. The tramway was constructed as authorised, with an overall length of 1,674 yards of which 1,102 yards was single track and the balance comprised passing loops, terminating at the Oldham boundary. The cost of permanent way construction was £9,731. 11*s.* 1*d.* (£400,000), and overhead equipment £1,078. 10*s.* 6*d.* (£45,000).

Oldham knew that Druitt was to inspect the Huddersfield extension from Elland to West Vale, which was only a few miles away across the Pennines, on Friday, 29th May 1914 and suggested that he covered Grains Bar also on that day, or on the Saturday. This was apparently not possible for the inspection took place on Whit Tuesday, 2nd June; possibly Druitt spent the holiday weekend in the North.

A speed limit of 12 miles an hour was allowed except for an eight mile an hour section between Sholver Lane and Grafton Street on the inward journey. A compulsory stop was required on the inward journey at Sholver Lane, and in both directions at the curve at the Besom Hill brickworks. For the last 150 yards the paving of the road between and outside the rails had not been completed so the trams were confined to a walking pace on this section until the work was done

The section was formally opened on Wednesday afternoon and the existing service from Hollinwood to Moorside was extended to Grains Bar the next morning, 4th June, with cars leaving Hollinwood at the hour and half hour. The takings on the Moorside – Grains Bar section were £123. 11*s.* 8½*d.* (£5,100) to 14th June, but declined to £105. 3*s.* 0½*d.* (£4,400) in the following fortnight, and to only £38. 17*s.* 7*d.* (£1,600) in the two weeks to 9th August.

The centre poles in Union Street and redundant rails in Egerton Street were removed in October / November; in December a track was laid in Walshaw Place for shunting purposes. This was a curtailed version of the original scheme whereby it would have rejoined the main line in a double junction just beyond the fork to Lees Road.

Plate 54. A heavily loaded Oldham car ex. MET in West Street about to cross Rochdale Road on its way to the Market Place. *Photo, Dr. H. A. Whitcombe*

Plate 55. One of the former Middleton Electric Traction Company's cars, now in Oldham ownership, seen against the railway embankment at Mills Hill. *Photo, Dr. Hugh Nicol*

PROPOSED EXTENSION TO NEW HEY

NORTH of Crompton lay Milnrow Urban District which also bordered on Rochdale. The Milnrow Urban District Council Tramways Order 1910 authorised two tramways totalling one mile 1,371 yards in length, commencing in Rochdale Road, Firgrove, by a junction at the boundary of Milnrow and Rochdale, with a tramway authorised by the Rochdale Corporation Act 1900, passing south easterly, terminating in New Hey Road at its junction with Huddersfield Road. The contract for constructing the lines was placed with George Law, Kidderminster, on 21st June 1911. Rochdale had agreed terms for leasing these tramways on 15th September 1909. Rochdale had opened the section to Firgrove (Newbold Street) on 5th October 1904; this was extended to Kiln Lane, Milnrow, on 12th December 1911, and over the remaining stretch to New Hey on 1st March 1912, a route length of 3 miles 332 yards from Rochdale centre. Because of low bridges, only single deck cars could be used on this route.

Crompton contacted Oldham in July 1911 suggesting an extension from Shaw to meet the proposed Milnrow line but no action was forthcoming. However, in May 1914 Crompton raised the matter again. The distance from the Wren's Nest terminus at Shaw to the Milnrow boundary was 1 mile 170 yards. Crompton wanted Oldham to take a lease of this section if constructed by Crompton, and Rochdale would be asked to take a lease of the connecting length of 625 yards through Milnrow to the existing terminus at New Hey. Oldham promised to inspect the proposed route. Two months later Oldham accepted the manager's advice following inspection, not to entertain the proposal. Finally, on a further approach by Crompton in April 1918 the Oldham Tramways Committee agreed to recommend the council to take a lease subject to satisfactory terms. No powers were obtained for the proposed extension, the potential profitability of which was adversely affected by the post-war inflation, and then by the improving economics of bus operation. However more than 80 years after the original proposal, an electric tramway connection between Shaw and New Hey will be made when the railway line from Manchester to Oldham and Rochdale is converted to Metrolink operation.

Plate 56. This original open top tram was fitted with an Oldham design top cover in November 1904. It is seen at the Chadderton Road terminus operating on the route to Shaw.

Photo, Courtesy Mrs. Pat Hyde

Plate 57. A Manchester balcony car approaches Mumps on its way to Waterhead about 1927. The four following views also date from the same period. *Photo, Lilywhite Ltd*

Plate 58. Car 39 operating on the circular route in Union Street.
Photo, Lilywhite Ltd

Plate 59. High Street showing car No. 72 on route 1, Hollinwood–Waterhead, in effect a short working of route 20.
Photo, Lilywhite Ltd

Plate 60. Rebuilt car No. 40 seen in Manchester Street, on its way to Lees about 1927.
Photo, Lilywhite Ltd

AN INTERNAL INQUIRY

On 7th May 1914, the Committee dismissed the Hollinwood works superintendent because of incompetence and gave him a month's wages in lieu of notice. Allegations made by the former employee led to criticism of the administration of the department by a councillor at the council meeting on 3rd June. The sequel was a meeting of the Tramways Committee on 14th July which lasted from 4.00 p.m. until 12.45 a.m. the next day, to consider in detail the various charges made.

These related to the prices paid for materials including tramway jacks, distance collars, trolley-heads, gear cases, the rewinding of armatures, magnetic track brakes, controllers, copper strip, axle brasses, an alleged defective truck, and unsatisfactory timber and chilled wheels. The charges seem to have been based largely if not wholly on claims made by the former employee and were refuted by the information elicited at the inquiry from Mr. Dugdale and from suppliers as appropriate. It was also alleged that the General Manager did not visit the Hollinwood works sufficiently often to judge the capabilities of the workforce or the problems entailed. The Committee strongly deprecated "the action of the late works superintendent in checking the movements of the General Manager, as it was no part of his duty to do so. Especially do they condemn the deputising of this timekeeping to some other man during the works superintendent's absence on holiday".

It was also claimed that a slipper brake supplied by C. H. Spencer of Gargrave (the patentee) for trial purposes was in a defective condition and cost £20 to fit. Mr. Spencer attended the hearing and said that the brake was in perfect condition but could not understand why it had cost £20 to fit. He was prepared to fit any number of brakes at £5 (£210) a set. The Committee considered that the works cost for fitting the brakes was exceedingly high. The brake had been obtained after the Salem Brow accident in 1912.

Satisfactory explanations were also forthcoming regarding allegations about "useless stores", and an alleged defective truck supplied by the United Electric Car Company.

Plate 61. Car No. 124 in High Street showing the Town Hall on the right. *Photo, Lilywhite Ltd*

Plate 62. A scene in High Street about 1920 as car No. 27 on the Manchester route approaches the Town Hall.

Plate 63. A scene at the Summit terminus during the dispute with Royton showing Rochdale tram 92 dating from 1926 and an Oldham bus. *Photo, Hall*

Plate 64. Another scene at the Summit terminus, this time showing Rochdale 87 and Oldham 22. The joint through service between the two towns ceased because Oldham was introducing top covered cars and these could not pass under the low railway bridge adjacent to Rochdale station. Despite exhaustive research it has not been possible to establish the date of cessation but it would seem likely to have been in December 1917. The headroom was increased by lowering the road in the 1920s thus enabling double deck cars to operate, but the through route was not reinstated.

Photo, Courtesy Roy Brook

WARTIME OPERATION

AN extraordinary series of collisions occurred on Tuesday afternoon, 21st September 1915 when tram No. 90 descending Werneth Brow got out of control; fortunately, it had no passengers. The tram left the rails and ran 30 or 40 yards on the setts: it struck a lorry laden with bales of cotton and then collided with a lorry belonging to the Great Central Railway Company, afterwards hitting a lorry carrying yarn. It then caught tram No. 92 on its way to Waterhead before colliding with a Ford motor van against which it came to rest. Not surprisingly the road was blocked for a considerable time.

As the effects of the war, which had started on 4th August 1914, were progressively felt, Oldham, in common with other tramway operators, experienced increasingly onerous operating conditions. Apart from the loss of manpower to the armed forces which, combined with material shortages, presented problems in maintaining services, there were the effects of air-raid precautions to contend with. Regulations regarding the latter seem to have been very much a local matter and were the cause of an unusual case in the Manchester Courts on 4th November 1915. Oldham Corporation was summoned for unlawfully having a light on one of its trams of "greater brightness than was necessary for public safety".

The Oldham tram had been seen in Oldham Road, Newton Heath on the evening of 20th October displaying a bright headlight which was not shaded in any way. Mr. Dugdale attended as chief witness for Oldham and said that the lighting restrictions were not then applicable to Oldham, but Failsworth through which the trams passed, was very badly lighted. Oldham wanted to do everything that was right but did not think it would be safe to reduce the lighting of the cars further. Mr. Dugdale said the car in question was an emergency car which had to be sent out hurriedly. It was pointed out that since the summons Oldham had subdued the headlights on the trams and there was now no cause for complaint. The bench having been satisfied on this point dismissed the case.

Meanwhile in March 1915 the Committee had inspected at Hollinwood some of the older trams which needed attention; this was not possible due to the lack of facilities caused by delays in completion of the depot extension then in progress. It was decided to send six of the oldest cars to the United Electric Car Company at Preston for repair. To compound the problems caused by the delayed building work, the extension when completed was taken over by Ferranti Limited, whose premises were adjacent, and who were then producing munitions, for shell storage; it was not returned to Oldham until July 1919.

In September 1916 it was decided to send a further eight cars to Preston for repair and overhaul and for six of them to be fitted with top covers. A pair of tram bogies was sold to Blackpool at this time, presumably from the former bogie car No. 3 which had been taken out of service in 1913 and the body used at Glodwick yard by the permanent way department.

By January 1916 there were 60 women employees on the trams and the Committee congratulated Mr. Dugdale on the suitability of the uniforms, which had been made to a design which he had registered. However, at a meeting on 24th February, it was reported that an account exceeding £400 (£12,000) had been incurred for the women's uniforms which had been ordered from the usual supplier of the men's uniforms, but without competitive tendering. The Committee expressed "its great astonishment and disapproval of the manager's action". The Committee also informed Mr. Dugdale that it was exceedingly dissatisfied with his conduct and management of the affairs of the department generally. It was decided that he should be asked to resign, to take effect in three months, and that he should be given until 1st March to comply. On this date, Dugdale duly resigned and his resignation was accepted at a meeting of the full Committee on the same day. He was paid four months salary and "relieved of all further duties in connection with the department". Perhaps there had been some substance in the 1914 allegations after all.

He was succeeded on 18th April by Percy Priestly, the general manager and engineer of Mexborough and Swinton Tramways Company out of 47 applicants at a salary of £400 (£12,000) a year rising by £50 annual increments to £500 (£15,000). His tenure of office was to prove relatively brief for he resigned in April 1918, on being appointed deputy general manager of Liverpool Corporation Tramways. Oldham then immediately appointed William Chamberlain, one of the Corporation's electrical engineers, to take over, again at a salary of £400 (£8,700) a year (but worth less because of inflation) rising by two annual increments to £500 (£11,000). In June 1919 the Committee was informed that Chamberlain was one of three candidates selected for the vacant managership at Hull Corporation Tramways at a salary of £800 (£16,000). It was agreed to increase his salary from £450 to £700 and then by two annual increments of £50 to £800 provided he undertook to stay for at least five years.

From time to time weather conditions exacerbated the difficulties under which the department was striving to maintain services under war time conditions. Particular problems arose in December 1916 as a result of fog and heavy snow storms. In a two week period the department lost 900 car miles due to fog and 520 car miles due to snow. There was a heavy fall of snow on the night of the 18th causing varying amounts of dislocation but most notably on the Moorside to Grains Bar section which was not reopened for a week.

On the night of the 15th a wagon ran into some houses near the White Hart Inn, Royton, blocking the line and disrupting the service, as a result of which there was a very severe collision between trams 37 and 95. Many trams had broken lifeguards because of the snow, and problems with motor leads arising from the salt which had been put on the track. In a two week period sickness caused the loss of 2,690 working hours, equivalent to the absence of 48 employees for a week, a serious situation given the impossibility of finding alternative workers.

Mr. Priestly pointed out that a lot of delay had arisen because a tower wagon which had been sent to Moorside had got stuck in the snow and much time had been spent trying to free it, instead of the men continuing on foot. As a result of this it was agreed to buy a motor car so that employees could be moved quickly when needed for emergencies.

On Monday, 8th January 1917 there was another heavy fall of snow but all tracks were cleared apart from the Moorside to Grains Bar section where the snow had drifted to four and five feet deep in places and the telephone wires were down; the current was cut off until the tracks could be cleared.

At this time there were nine cars operating the joint service between Oldham and Manchester, comprising five Manchester and four Oldham cars. This number would need to be increased to 13 to introduce a 10 minute service which the manager thought desirable since the train fare had recently been increased. However, Manchester was unable to agree with this proposal. Another suggestion was to run non-stop cars to Hollinwood but the Mayor suggested that the previous car "no matter how much of a start it got" would soon be caught on the journey. There was also the problem of Board of Trade compulsory stops.

The end of January saw yet more snow and interruption to services, particularly on the Moorside–Grains Bar section which was closed for a week. One effect of the snow, bearing in mind the hilly nature of the main roads in Oldham, was that motor vehicles were fouling the tracks because of the state of the roads; at one stage there were seven motor vehicles stranded between Royal Oak and Werneth fire station. There were at least three instances of trams towing vehicles up Werneth Brow but the manager banned this practice because of the strain on the tram motors. Mr. Priestly pointed out that the road was extremely slippery on this stretch and it had been necessary to use a lot of sand in assisting the motor vehicles. Although the police gave every assistance in trying to keep the road clear it was "really impossible to regulate the traffic owing to the state of the roads", and he thought that the Carrying & Cleansing Department should sand this part of the track more regularly. In a general discussion on this problem the manager said that if drivers thought they would be helped they would travel on the track knowing that the tram drivers would tow them out of the way.

In a further report in February Mr. Priestly referred to the large amount of absence through sickness arising from the atrocious weather, and the inevitable cuts in services; he pointed out that the services in Manchester and Salford had been considerably reduced for the same reason. In addition to the time lost by sickness there was the state of the track and delays caused by other vehicular traffic. The previous Saturday he had arranged for the snow ploughs to run throughout the night in order to keep the tracks clear; services between Summit and Hathershaw, and between Shaw and Werneth had to be cut short because of a water main burst at Longsight, Royton.

At a meeting on 22nd March the manager was able to report a general improvement in conditions. However, the Grains Bar section had been out of action for four days because severe gales had brought down all the telephone wires. A welcome item was the chief constable's agreement that trams could now be run without shades on the inside lights. This relaxation came about because it had been pointed out that the company trams running between Hathershaw and Ashton, which was under

Plate 65. A Manchester car approaches the ascent of Manchester Road near Hollinwood. *Photo, Chas Wilkinson*

the jurisdiction of the Lancashire County Council, ran with unshaded lights; the police authority had agreed to this because the current could be cut off at any time requisite. The Oldham cars were, however, operating with some 48 candle power instead of the normal 150 candle power, but the Chairman was pleased that the undertaking was now to get the full benefit of the cost of the current used!

At the meeting on 14th June 1917, Mr. Priestly was able to report record receipts over the Whitsuntide holiday period. At that time 93 trams were available for service ("complete with equipment") and of these 90 were in service; of the other three one was in the paint shop, one was dismantled for overhaul and the third was being overhauled and fitted with a top cover at English Electric, Preston. Traffic to Grains Bar was particularly heavy; some motormen worked 16 and 17 hours without a break for a meal. It was also added that some thanks were due to the railway companies for increasing their fares so that people would not travel far from home. On a less welcome note, there was heavy traffic to Ashton by sightseers following a devastating munitions explosion at Hooley Hill Chemical & Rubber Co. At the end of the year double deck trams replaced single deck vehicles on the circular route, with increased receipts.

In January 1918, a passenger descending from the upper deck of a car was hit by a falling trolley head; as a result the fastenings of the trolley heads were altered to prevent a recurrence. In February, as a result of a mishap in the Market Place the guard wires were pulled down, completely disorganising the whole service. The manager pointed out that there was constant trouble because of the large number of guard wires over the Market Place crossings and so the current feed arrangements were being changed with the result that any further cases of wires being brought down would affect only the Market Place and not other routes. Also this month, Bolton's illuminated tram toured the system in Tank Week, an event promoting savings to help finance the war.

At the meeting held on 30th May 1918, Mr. Chamberlain, the new manager, reported exceptionally heavy traffic over the previous fortnight which included the Whitsuntide holiday. Assisted by fare increases, receipts for the week to 26th May were £4,362. 13*s.* 2*d.* (£92,000) against £2,814. 5*s.* 9*d.* (£67,000) a year earlier. There had been particularly heavy traffic over the weekend to the termini at Grains Bar, Hathershaw, Lees and Waterhead, which gave access to the countryside. On the Saturday morning, there had been a long queue at Hathershaw waiting for the Ashton cars which gave access to Gee Cross, Mottram and Werneth Low. Restrictions on railway traffic were "so drastic that travelling for pleasure in some districts is almost forbidden" and the trams "leading to the edge of the country" had never been so highly appreciated as in recent days. The railways were not taking bookings to Belle Vue, Manchester, and so there was very heavy traffic on the through route to the city. A particularly pleasing feature was a record established by the works department when on one Saturday no trams had suffered a defect, a situation which had never arisen previously on such a busy day.

As the war neared its end, inadequate coal supplies restricted electricity generation, and the Government called on users to curtail consumption. Oldham responded by reducing the Sunday morning services between 10.00 a.m. and 2.30 p.m. These were reduced to one car on each section except Middleton Road which had none, thus requiring only six tram crews instead of the normal service requiring 27, and on occasions, 34. In October it was reported that mileage had been reduced compared with the previous year by 6%, whereas energy usage was down between 7% and 8%. The manager was given permission to make further reductions by curtailing the number of cars outside the peak periods.

In June 1918, Oldham agreed with Manchester's suggestion to provide a freight tram in connection with the parcels traffic between Manchester and Oldham. The terms proved to be onerous to Oldham and in January 1919 Manchester was asked to reduce Oldham's contribution by £10 a month. This Manchester agreed to do. At the same time the scale of charges for parcels traffic was revised, the lowest charge being 3*d.* (24p) for parcels up to 14 lbs. The parcels car visited Oldham two or three times a day, and over a period Oldham collected 10,000 parcels compared with 61,000 by Manchester. In the months to March 1919, Oldham lost £814 (£16,000) on the parcels operation.

WINTER UNIFORMS FOR WOMEN

The accompanying illustrations show the neat and serviceable uniforms that have been provided for winter wear by the 60 women at work on the Oldham Corporation tramcars. The garments are made to a design registered by Mr. J. W. Dugdale, the general manager, who has been congratulated by the Tramways Committee upon the suitability of the outfit. Already it has been inspected by managers from other tramways.

Uniform worn while at work.

Off-duty Uniform of Conductors at Oldham.

From *The Tramway and Railway World*, 13th January 1916.

Plate 66. Manchester balcony car 726 on the single track section of Yorkshire Street on its way to Waterhead about 1930.
Photo, J. Valentine

CHADDERTON CONNECTION

OVER the years there were continuing complaints about waiting times at the Chadderton-Oldham boundary when passengers wished to transfer from one system to the other. A lot of these arose from the fact that the operating frequencies on the two sections were different. However, it was also a common complaint that one tram would leave just as another was approaching. Eventually, Chadderton council wrote to both the Middleton Company and to Oldham regarding the state of affairs.

The manager of the Traction Company commented: "I need hardly say that the complaint referred to is one which I have used every endeavour to avoid. Our mens' instructions are clear and emphatic. They are not to leave the terminus when a car of another system is approaching until they see if there are any passengers on that car desiring to go forward on their car. This order is to be carried out even if the car is late. I have punished many conductors for dereliction of this order, and have even discharged them for it on several occasions. It is only when specific instances are brought to my notice that I am able to deal with the individual concerned, and I shall be glad if any one who has cause for complaint in this regard will report same to me giving time and car No. if possible, and I will then deal severely with the man concerned. I am using strong remedies with the conductors and hope a better state of affairs will result in future".

Plate 67. An early 1920s scene in Shaw. *Photo, A. J. Lees*

Mr. Chamberlain wrote for Oldham:

"I am in receipt of your letter of the 17th inst. regarding running the Oldham cars in connection with the Middleton cars, and I assure you that this matter will receive early attention".

One councillor thought the reply satisfactory but another claimed that he caught only one out of six cars which he wished to catch. "The cars were not run to time. They did not consider any one. People were continually complaining about cars passing them. They did exactly what they wanted. Middleton people were complaining about the system just as much as Chadderton residents and he thought they ought to get into touch with Middleton". After other councillors had vented their feelings, the matter was allowed to drop.

Plate 68. In the late 1930s many local tramway scenes were captured by tramway enthusiasts. This and the following photographs fall into this category. Car 18 climbs Manchester Road on its way to Shaw. A tram stop sign can be seen on the tram standard. *Photo, H. B. Priestley*

EARLY BUSES

THIS is a convenient point at which to relate Oldham's excursion in the field of bus operation. In December 1912, the Committee agreed to purchase two Tilling Stevens petrol electric buses and in January there was a trial run with a Daimler bus in the Coppice area and to Grains Bar to demonstrate its hill climbing ability. The buses duly arrived and by moving the sand dryer from the Copster Hill premises to Glodwick Road it was possible to garage them at Copster Hill. A service commenced on 12th May 1913 operating from the Town Hall along Clegg Street, Union Street, Union Street West, Werneth Hall Road, Coppice Street, Wellington Road, and Windsor Road to College Road running weekdays only, at a fare of 1d. It will be recalled that powers for tramways in the Coppice Street area had been considered in 1908. In view of the new bus service the Union Street West tram service was discontinued after Saturday 10th May. Buses also ran to Grains Bar on Saturdays and Sundays at the manager's discretion. In June, it was decided to buy another bus as a reserve in case of breakdowns. Problems were experienced on the steepest part of Werneth Hall Road near Lee Street so the route was varied from Union Street via Napier Street East and St. Thomas's Street North to Werneth Hall Road, probably commencing on 15th September; the following month the service reverted to the original route.

In August 1914 Oldham agreed with Saddleworth to provide a bus service between Grains Bar and Denshaw during Wakes week and on 16th August 1915 revised the original service to operate between Coppice and the General Post Office in Union Street, now the Local Studies Library. To make this service more economic Oldham purchased a second hand single deck bus body for use on one of the Coppice vehicle chassis in February 1917 and in May sold two buses (registration numbers BU11 and BU402) to Warrington, leaving one vehicle for the Coppice service. A body ex a Tilling Stevens was fitted to an electric chassis. Later in the year the Coppice bus service was operated with coal gas but in December this was found to be unsatisfactory. An order was placed with Electro Mobile Company Limited, Leeds, for a chassis for an electrically driven vehicle but in the following February, the Ministry of Munitions refused a permit for the purchase of this chassis. The immediate reaction was to discontinue the Coppice service, but second thoughts prevailed and it continued to operate. Finally, in August 1919, in view of the heavy wear and tear, Oldham concluded that two vehicles were not sufficient to maintain a reliable service and a third was needed. Taken in conjunction with the fact that the service was continuing to lose money it was later decided to discontinue it, and on 8th December, the Union Street West (Lee Street) and Waterhead tram service was reinstated. The electric bus was sold to Belgrave Mills Company Limited and a Tilling Stevens chassis to Central Motor (Oldham) Limited.

On 1st December, the tram service between Werneth Fire Station and Shaw, Beal Lane, was extended to Shaw, Wren's Nest, following complaints of obstruction at Beal Lane; it was further extended to operate between Shaw and Hollinwood on 31st January 1921, to relieve congestion between Hollinwood and the Fire Station.

Plate 69. No. 84 at Hathershaw terminus ready for the return journey to Summit.

THE OLDHAM AND CHADDERTON TRAMWAYS ACT, 1919

THE 1909 Act had allowed five years for the construction of the lines authorised, and this period expired in August 1914. By June 1914 all but tramway No. 4, the line from Manchester Road along Oxford Street to the Chadderton boundary, had been constructed, and it was agreed to let the powers for this line lapse. However, towards the end of the war there was a request from the Alliance Aeroplane Factory at Gorse Hill, Chadderton, for a bus or other service to the plant. The Tramways Committee proposed that Oldham should obtain Board of Trade permission for a tramway along Oxford Street to the boundary to connect with a proposed line in Chadderton. However, shortly afterwards the Armistice was signed and the Ministry wrote to Chadderton suggesting that the tramway should be deferred "since it was anticipated that work will have to cease on aircraft assembly". Chadderton was anxious to see a route into the district via Oxford Street and powers for this were obtained under the Oldham and Chadderton Tramways Act, 1919. Apart from re-authorising the line in Oxford Street which now comprised 405 yards of single track and 207 yards of double track, compared with 325 yards and 287 yards respectively in the 1909 Act, it also authorised a section wholly in Chadderton. This was along Block Lane, Wash Brook, Butler Green, Thompson Lane and Whitegate Lane as proposed by Chadderton in 1908; it was 1,562 yards long comprising 684 yards single and 878 yards of double track.

On 11th December the Oldham Tramway Committee walked over the proposed tramway route, meeting representatives from Chadderton council at the boundary, who accompanied them to Eaves Lane, location of the aircraft plant mentioned earlier. The outcome was that it was agreed to start work in February 1921, with the object of finishing not later than September of that year, when the powers lapsed.

However, there was renewed interest in buses and on 17th February the Committee toured the proposed tramway in a demonstration bus provided by Bristol Carriage & Tramways Company. The Committee do not seem to have been very impressed because the manager was instructed to pursue details of operation by trolleybuses. Later in the year an independent operator moved in, with a bus service between Rhodes Bank and Wash Brook, competing over part of this route with Oldham trams.

A year's extension of time to construct the Chadderton line (the maximum permissible) was sought and granted in 1921 – and in the subsequent three years. Over this period, motorbus development was such that this type of transport was eventually used on the route instead of trams.

Plate 70. Tram No. 124, destination Hollinwood, is held up by a Manchester tram as it leaves Market Place, Oldham.
Photo, H. B. Priestley

JOINT SERVICE TO ASHTON

A FURTHER extension to the route mileage though not to the mileage owned by Oldham took place to the south of the Borough. Under the terms of the Tramways Act, a local authority could purchase tramways in its area after the elapse of 21 years. This period expired in the case of the Oldham, Ashton and Hyde Electric Tramway Limited in 1917 but recognising difficulties caused by wartime conditions, the Special Powers (Extension of Time) Act had been enacted to give an extended period in such situations. Proposed lines in Oldham had been struck out of the company's Bill on Oldham's objections. The Act authorising the tramway had barred the company from making any junction with the Oldham Corporation lines, then operated by the Bury, Rochdale and Oldham company. Since the company did not operate in Oldham, the northern terminus being at the southern boundary on Ashton Road near Fir Tree Avenue, Oldham was not involved in the purchase. After protracted negotiations followed by arbitration arising from the parties' failure to agree terms, the undertaking was duly purchased by the local authorities concerned, and a connection was made with the Oldham tramways.

Oldham considered a report on through running with Ashton at its meeting of 23rd June 1921. The principle of through running had been agreed with Ashton before Ashton and the other authorities concerned had purchased the system. Councillor Shorrocks referred to an item in the report that the track between Ashton and the Oldham boundary was in such a state that it was not considered advisable to run double deck cars over it. He took that to mean that the track was not in a good condition. The manager agreed and said that Ashton had decided to substitute a double track as far as possible without delay but intended to maintain a service whilst the relaying was taking place.

Because of long stretches of single track each side of Bardsley Brow (the boundary between Limehurst Rural District and Ashton), the frequency could not be greater than 10 minutes which would entail the use of four Ashton and two Oldham trams. It was felt to be impractical to run through cars into Oldham Market Place. It was pointed out that under existing rates Ashton would charge 3*d.* to carry a 56 lb parcel to Oldham whereas in the opposite direction Oldham would charge 6*d.* (47p), an anomaly which would be dealt with. A service between the Star Inn and Ashton, Market Place, operated jointed by Oldham and Ashton commenced on Saturday 2nd July 1921, under route No. 14. The Oldham service between Hathershaw and Summit continued to operate. The expressed intention to extend the Ashton service to Summit was never realised.

Plate 71. Manchester tram 287 descends Yorkshire Street about 1930 on its way to Waterhead. *Photo, Valentine's Series*

Plate 72. Car 123 stands at Hollinwood ready for departure on the short working 11 service to Market Place.

Plate 73. This view at Hathershaw shows in the gap between the houses beyond the tram the turning circle for the Ashton trolleybuses. The destination indicator on number 8 reads Summit for Rochdale but the trolley has not yet been turned.

Plate 74. Manchester 104 and Oldham 125 at the Waterhead terminus with the open country beyond. The terminus was originally double-track but following relaying in 1920 there was a single track in the middle of the road which 125 has just left, (on 10th August 1935), thus facilitating the passage of other road traffic.

Photo, A. M. Gunn

ACCIDENT IN COPSTER HILL ROAD

AN accident occurred on 7th June 1921, in Copster Hill Road when a tram ran backwards. This matter attracted the interest of the Ministry of Transport which had taken over the responsibilities of the Board of Trade for tramway matters in 1919. The Ministry suggested that Oldham should fit sanders which would drop sand behind the wheels. The sanders on the Oldham cars dropped the sand in front of the wheels but this was of no benefit if the car was running backwards. Oldham relied on the conductor to use the peddle at his end to drop sand in such circumstances.

Mr. Chamberlain disagreed with the Ministry's suggestion to fix an apparatus at the front of the car which the driver could operate to cover cars running away either forwards or backwards, believing that the simpler the work of the driver could be made, the better. The Ministry responded by pointing out that it was the common practice of tramways undertakings to print rules and regulations for the guidance of their employees in cases of emergencies. In the case of Oldham, given the gradients on the system: "... a free and immediate use of sand was necessary in the case of a car getting out of control and running backwards. For this purpose either the use of a double-ended sander, or an arrangement whereby the conductor should always travel on the rear platform with the said sand peddle in operation, was necessary. Unless one of these alternatives was adopted the Ministry would be unable to regard the action of the Corporation as being conducive to public safety".

The chairman pointed out that if the latter alternative was adopted say in Middleton Road the conductor would not have time to collect the fares. A trolley boy would then become necessary on these cars. Sensibly, the committee felt it would be fairly simple to devise something which the driver could easily operate, and the manager was asked to find a solution. Eventually, on 1st March 1923 Mr. Chamberlain demonstrated the effectiveness of tram brakes 'and other devices for public safety', including a mechanical back sander, on the Grains Bar route. The back sander had been invented by Thomas Curry, a foreman at Hollinwood depot who was paid £80 for the right to install it on all the Oldham trams when the Ministry approved its use.

In April 1923, Lees requested an extension along Huddersfield Road from the existing terminus at Waterhead through Lees to its boundary with Springhead at Austerlands (Thorpe Lane). After considering the proposal, Oldham decided in July to defer the matter for 12 months but eventually provided a bus service. The proposed extension represented a portion of tramway 4 of the Saddleworth and Springhead Act of 1902 and included a short stretch of Springhead territory between Oldham and Lees.

Plate 75. Car 44 at Summit terminus on 10th August 1935, with the destination Hathershaw for Ashton.

Photo, A. M. Gunn

POST SERVICE

FOLLOWING an approach by the General Post Office, Manchester had introduced a postal service on selected tram routes commencing on Monday 5th November 1923. Oldham was also approached by the Post Office but was not prepared to accept the terms suggested, namely, that the operator should provide the boxes, with the Post Office supplying the locks and keys. On the routes into Manchester a mail box was provided on the journey arriving in the centre of Manchester at about 9.30 p.m. Eventually on 6th April 1925 this facility was extended to Oldham, departing Waterhead at 8.25 arriving in Stevenson Square, Manchester at 9.30.

In March 1927, the Oldham Postmaster suggested a letter facility from Shaw to Oldham. Alderman Cheetham, who had (as a Councillor until 1926) been Chairman of the Committee since November 1916 mentioned that on a previous occasion "the Post Office notion was that the tramways department should bear the cost, take responsibility, and not draw any return for the conveyance of the mails, so they dropped the matter" It was stated that Huddersfield was paid £25 (£600) a year for 110 boxes, Manchester £4 (£97) a box, and in other instances there was no payment. Oldham thought that there was a difficulty in taking responsibility for the mail; when the box got nearly full it was possible to snatch letters out of it. Terms were discussed with the Post Office but no action was taken.

The postal service continued operating Mondays to Fridays until Friday 1st September 1939 when it was discontinued because of the war which started on 3rd September. The postal tram was indicated by a stencil reading POST CAR in place of the route number.

Plate 76. Also on 10th August 1935, car No. 67 at the Hathershaw terminus. *Photo, A. M. Gunn*

Plate 77. The Summit terminus seen in August 1936 with car 122 on the 7 route showing destination Hathershaw for Ashton. This car is equipped with truck covers.

Photo, E. Fielding

Plate 78. On 2nd August 1937 Oldham 7 turns from Lever Street into Stevenson Square, Manchester, and is followed by Manchester tram 360 on the 26B short working to Audenshaw on the Ashton route and 173 on the 26 route to Ashton.
Photo, A. M. Gunn

Plate 79. Oldham 5 turns from Oldham Road into Great Ancoats Street, Manchester, followed by a Manchester bus on 21st August, 1937.
Photo, A. M. Gunn

Plate 80. No. 5 inward bound to Manchester in Oldham Road at Thompson Street on 7th April, 1938.

NORTH WESTERN ROAD CAR COMPANY LTD

A DIFFICULT situation arose in January 1924 when the North Western Road Car Company notified its intention to operate buses from Oldham to Delph, from Oldham to Grasscroft and Greenfield Station via Lees and between Uppermill, Delph and Diggle. The Watch Committee was in favour of granting licences to North Western but the Tramways Committee commented unfavourably on "the unreasonableness of private companies being allowed to compete with municipal tramway services". It was decided to call the attention of the Municipal Tramways Association to this development with the object of co-ordinating a response by the municipal operators.

Oldham's next move, on 17th July, was to order five one-man operated 24 seat buses from Leyland Motor Company. A trial run in one of these took place on 31st July, over a proposed route including the Coppice district, but within the borough. At this time, Oldham did not have any powers to operate buses beyond its boundary but these were granted in the Oldham Corporation Act, 1925.

At its meeting on 24th September 1924 the Watch Committee considered an application from the company regarding proposed services from Oldham to Huddersfield and Halifax, and the route to be taken within Oldham. Mr. Chamberlain said the tramways department did not claim preferential treatment but given that it had 17½ million 1*d.* (10p) fares out of 36 million passengers a year it had a strong claim for transport between street and street within Oldham as compared with long distance transport. He said that the cars on the circular route ought to travel via George Street and through the town but congestion did not allow this; the Ashton route cars ran only to the Star Inn for the same reason.

The situation in Oldham was difficult owing to the narrow streets and allowing the buses to run to the centre of the town would superimpose services on a municipal service which was both cheap and adequate. He thought that when people were carried eight or ten miles it would not impose any hardship by requiring them to change at the Oldham boundary, and that the buses should be excluded. In support he said that passengers within the borough had to change trams and the company services were town-to-town and not street-to-street services. If services were increased in the way proposed, congestion would be very serious; on a Saturday evening 123 trams passed through Market Place within an hour. He thought therefore that the bus services ought to terminate at the boundary; Oldham would very seriously consider working in conjunction with the company in the provision of waiting rooms, connections and through tickets.

Mr. Cardwell, the Manager of North Western, said they were endeavouring to link towns and villages. They had tried running to tram termini and it was not satisfactory because whereas the trams were at a five to ten minute frequency the buses ran only every hour or so and if the tram was a minute or two late the bus was missed.

The Mayor, Councillor J.K. Cheetham, who was also the chairman of the Tramways Committee, said the company came in and ran services where it liked. Legislation tied the hands of the municipality and placed conditions on corporation trams with which omnibus companies had not to contend. Oldham was obliged to carry workmen at a ½*d.* (5p) a mile and to run trams at regular times whether they paid or not.

At the time of the meeting the North Western buses arrived and departed to the rear of Oldham church and it was pointed out that on the way out there were four right angle turns in a very short distance. The meeting agreed that the buses could start from St. Peter's Street, leaving via Clegg Street and Union Street to Mumps Bridge, returning by Yorkshire Street. The proposed Huddersfield route was via Delph, Marsden, Slaithwaite, Meltham and Lockwood; the Halifax route would be via Grains Bar, Denshaw, Rishworth and Ripponden. Initially there would be about six journeys daily on each route.

The following March the Watch Committee was somewhat surprised by an application from North Western for licences for 129 buses to ply in the borough, additional to 20 which has already been granted. North Western said that the move was to enable the company to allocate buses between the areas in which it operated and it was proposed to licence 129 for some 30 districts altogether. Generally speaking North Western would not operate more buses than the number of licensed conductors, which was then 17. Oldham granted the application until May when the existing licences were due to be reviewed, so that the whole 149 could be considered together.

Plate 81. Market Place Oldham about 1939 following redevelopment.

Photo, Valentine's Series

Plate 82. Trams for Oldham normally used the centre of three tracks in Stevenson Square, Manchester, as shown here. The oval notice in the shelter on the right reads “Intending passengers must form a queue and board cars in that order. Persons not complying may be prosecuted”.

Photo, A. M. Gunn

LICENCE PROBLEM

OLDHAM ordered a further five leyland buses, subsequently reduced to four, seating 28, on 5th October 1924. On Monday 15th December, Oldham introduced a bus service from Hollinwood Railway Station along Manchester Road, Chamber Road, Coppice Street, Napier Street East, Union Street West, Union Street and Mumps to Mumps Bridge, thus covering the area served by the original pre-war service. The Manager had applied for a licence to operate this service and the matter came before the Watch Committee two days later. At this point, Councillor Cheetham said he was withdrawing the application on behalf of Mr. Chamberlain, on the grounds that the Tramways Committee was under no obligation to seek licences and had the power to run the buses without.

The Chief Constable said that the buses were running without licences and under the 1909 Act they had no power to do so. The Act stated that Oldham could run buses for transport purposes, but could not ply for hire. The Town Clerk said that he had considered the matter carefully and concluded that the buses must be licensed. Councillor Cheetham then asked if that ruling did not govern trams also. He claimed that if the Watch Committee had done its duty in regard to tramcars every tram on the streets should be licensed according to the ruling. The Committee had allowed that to go by default and there had been no licence for a tram and consequently licences were not required for buses. The Watch Committee Chairman suggested that Councillor Cheetham's argument was equivalent to saying that if a man got drunk and was let off by a policeman and then got drunk again, the policeman would have no right to lock him up.

After a lengthy and heated discussion during which it was suggested that the buses were causing an obstruction at Mumps, Councillor Cheetham invited prosecution. The Committee ultimately agreed that licences should be granted, to run over a route detailed by Councillor Cheetham.

At the Tramways Committee meeting the following day Councillor Cheetham submitted that the Watch Committee had no jurisdiction over them, and had approved something the Tramways Committee had not asked for. He was concerned that if traffic experience dictated that the buses should be transferred to another route, the Watch Committee could claim that the buses were licensed for a particular route. He said the Watch Committee might just as well pass a resolution that the tide must not come in at Blackpool.

In a long discussion the Town Clerk expressed the view that the Watch Committee had no inherent right to fix the routes, but they might be able to say it was undesirable to run in certain congested streets. Mr. Chamberlain said that the tramways being the expert operating authority, would best know as to what was dangerous. It was eventually decided to record in the minutes that there had been a discussion, and take no further action. General satisfaction at the performance of the bus service was expressed; it was mentioned that 2,146 passengers were carried on Tuesday and 2,284 on Wednesday.

A bus service was introduced between the Chadderton Road tram terminus and Moston on 28th February 1925, and on 16th March, the route of the Hollinwood–Mumps Bridge service was amended by curtailing it at the Hollinwood end to commence at the junction of Chapel Road and Manchester Road, and by an extension from Mumps through Bottom o'th' Moor along Greenacres Road to the terminus near Greenacres cemetery. At this time Oldham was operating five front-entrance single-deck buses seating 24 (increased to 26 at the end of the decade). The buses cost £5,075 (£125,000) and incurred a loss of £140 (£3,200) in the period to 25th March 1925.

New routes opened up over the next twelve months were Clegg Street Station - Middleton Junction, 1st August, Rhodes Bank - Butler Green, 20th August, Royton Railway Station - Failsworth, 29th August and Oldham Town Hall - Mossley (Brook Bottom) on 23rd January 1926. During this period the Chadderton Road - Moston service ceased. The bus fleet trebled by March 1926, the additional vehicles being the four Leyland 28 seat single-deck front-entrance buses ordered in October 1924, and six AEC double-deck vehicles with a capacity of 52; the latter, however, had not been put in service. The year's working saw an enhanced loss of £1,470. The ensuing twelve months saw two more AEC's delivered and also the first Guy vehicles, three double-deck vehicles seating 54 and two single-deck seating 32, all these being six wheeled buses, bringing the fleet to 22 vehicles.

In a new departure, a double-deck bus service was introduced operating alongside the trams between Summit and Hathershaw on 2nd April 1926; on 29th

September the service between Clegg Street Station and Middleton Junction was amended to operate between Star Inn and Middleton Junction. In the New Year a service was introduced between Oldham Town Hall and Manor Road on 1st January 1927 and on the 28th the Rhodes Bank and Butler Green service was amended to operate between Rhodes Bank and Coalshaw Green. The year's working saw the first profits from bus operation, £1,931.

Plate 83. Car 15 photographed by Mr. H. B. Priestley on 2nd August 1938 entering service from Walshaw depot. The following four photographs were also taken by Mr. Priestley on the same day.

Plate 84. Car 41 also leaving the depot, this time entering service on route No. 1.

OLDHAM CORPORATION ACT 1925

IN the early 1920s Oldham found it necessary to promote a General Act seeking further powers over its various activities and including in Part IV provisions relating to tramways, trolleybuses and motorbuses.

In its Bill, Oldham was seeking powers to acquire the Middleton Electric Traction Company. Rochdale pointed out to Oldham, in January 1925, that, together with Middleton and Chadderton, it had been negotiating the acquisition of the company. As a result of this approach, Oldham agreed to limit its proposed operations to the section from its Middleton Road terminus, the Chadderton boundary with Oldham, through Chadderton to the boundary with Middleton at Mills Hill and thence to Middleton Market Place, and probably to Rhodes. On this undertaking, Rochdale agreed to withdraw its opposition to Oldham's Bill. Lancashire County Council intimated that it, and probably other authorities adjacent to Oldham, opposed Oldham's application for powers to operate trolleybuses outside Oldham.

Under the subsequent Act, Oldham was given general powers to maintain, renew and alter its tramway system as necessary and also to construct the tramway authorised by the Oldham and Chadderton Tramways Order 1919, with the proviso that it should not be opened to traffic until the carriageway throughout its entire length had been widened by the reduction of the footpaths or otherwise, to a minimum width of 24 feet. The Chadderton tramway was to be completed within five years from the passing of the Act, or such further period as might be approved by the Minister of Transport.

Oldham was also empowered to purchase by agreement any, or all, of the tramways in Chadderton, Lees, Royton and Crompton on terms agreed with the prospective vendors. Oldham was also given authority to purchase the portion of the Middleton Electric Traction Company's undertaking in Chadderton from the company or any other owner on such terms as might be agreed, but only with the consent of Chadderton. Although the Act did not receive the Royal Assent until 7th August the Middleton powers were deemed to have been in operation from 1st July 1925.

Oldham was also given powers to operate trolleybuses from the boundary in Ashton Road, along that road, King Street, Wellington Street, Chaucer Street, Union Street and King Street to its junction with Wellington Street. With the consent of the Minister of Transport, Oldham was also enabled to operate trolleybuses along any thoroughfare in Oldham for which it was authorised to construct or work tramways. Additionally, with the consent of the Minister, by agreement with the Local Authority concerned, Oldham could also operate trolleybuses on any of the authorised tramways in Chadderton, Lees, Royton and Crompton.

Finally, the Act enabled Oldham to operate motorbuses for five miles beyond its boundary with the consent of the Local Authority concerned.

Plate 85. Pilcher car 217 destined for Stevenson Square showing, from the left, Oldham cars numbers 124, 9 and 128 in the Market Place.

THROUGH SERVICE TO MIDDLETON

CHAMBERLAIN resigned as manager in April 1925 on being appointed general manager of Leeds Corporation Tramways. He was succeeded by Clement Jackson aged 32, general manager of Keighley Corporation Tramways, from 34 applicants at a salary of £750 (£18,000). He took up his duties at the beginning of July and thus arrived on the scene as the tramways were being extended by the acquisition of the Middleton company's line in Chadderton, now related below.

This major event involved further extension of Oldham's route mileage but also extended its track mileage. It will be recalled that the local authorities in whose areas the Middleton Electric Traction Company was operating were empowered to purchase the undertaking after 25 years had elapsed from the commencement of the Light Railway Order – the operative date being 15th December 1923 – by giving six months notice of their intention to do so. The local authorities concerned were Chadderton, and the Boroughs of Middleton and Rochdale, the latter through its absorption of Castleton Urban District on 9th November 1900, the month in which construction commenced on the Castleton section. In January 1923 Chadderton informed Oldham of the situation pointing out that to acquire the company that year, each of the local authorities concerned had to pass a special resolution by 15th June 1923. The outcome was the following report from Chamberlain on 28th February 1923, to his committee:

"Middleton Light Railways Order 1898 to 1920

"In accordance with your instructions, I have given careful consideration to the question of leasing the existing light railway in the Chadderton and Middleton Districts.

"The committee will realise that owing to the request of the Chadderton Deputation, I have been unable to inspect the details of the system, or to make any close inquiries regarding the details of working to guide me in assessing the value of the property, and the probable revenue to be obtained in operating the section.

"I understand, however, that the line will require to be reconstructed within the next five years. This is a very important point for the Committee's consideration.

"Recently, I inspected the system of 'railless' traction in Birmingham, and although I am of opinion that tramcars are still the most effective and cheapest form of passenger road vehicle in densely populated districts as compared with other forms of present day vehicles, there is doubtless a wide field open for the operation of 'railless' vehicles.

"'Railless' vehicles will, in my opinion, supersede tramcars on single line routes in sparsely populated districts when these lines become due for reconstruction.

"The Committee is now reaching a sound financial position owing to the redemption of loans, the creation of assets out of revenue, and beneficial assets remaining in daily use which have been entirely written off the Capital Account. This position will, I trust, be reflected in the future by lower working and capital costs, with the consequent reduction in fares.

"For these reasons, and in the absence of what might be termed a higher policy of the Corporation in providing public utilities in outside Districts, I would recommend the Committee in approaching this matter to view the proposal from the commercial aspect, and, in the event of the line being taken over, to fix fares and stages in accordance with the actual cost to the Committee without regard to the fares and stages in operation on other sections of the Oldham Tramways."

Manchester operated a tramway from Manchester to Middleton and also a branch from Middleton to Middleton Junction, the lines in Middleton being owned by Middleton and leased to Manchester for 21 years expiring on 23rd December 1923. Manchester clearly had an interest in the future of the Middleton Electric Traction Company's system and hosted a meeting on 6th April 1923, at which the Middleton, Rochdale and Chadderton councils decided to consider the purchase of the tramway. They appointed Arthur Collins of Abingdon Street, Westminster as financial adviser and J. B. Hamilton, the Manager of Leeds Corporation Tramways, as technical advisor. However, the local authorities did not give the required six months notice for purchase in 1923.

In the accounts issued in June 1924, the directors of the company pointed out that statutory powers of purchase would not recur for seven years, but noted that the company could sell at any time by agreement, with the consent of the Minister of Transport. It is possible that the local authorities were influenced by the result of the arbitration in 1921 over the purchase of the Oldham, Ashton and

Hyde system which arose from the failure of the parties to agree on the purchase price. Given the Middleton company's financial situation they probably reasoned that they were in a good bargaining position.

At a meeting of the Middleton Council held on 29th April 1925, the negotiations which had taken place between Middleton and Manchester for a new 21 years lease of the Middleton lines, and proposals for the acquisition of the company's lines within the borough and subsequent lease to Manchester, were explained. The meeting approved a draft agreement with Manchester. It had previously been arranged that if the draft agreement was approved a deputation from Middleton, Rochdale and Chadderton would meet the directors of the company in London on 1st May to discuss the acquisition of the company. A sub-committee was empowered to take part in these negotiations, or alternatively to negotiate acquisition of the Middleton portion separately.

Agreement was reached for the purchase of the undertaking for a total of £79,000 (£1.9m) as from midnight, Monday 15th June, with an additional £3,500 (£85,000) for stores and spares. It was subsequently agreed that the tramway managers of Manchester, Rochdale and Oldham should decide the allocation of this amount between the three purchasing authorities and should operate the system through an acting manager pending the transfer to Middleton, Rochdale and Chadderton of the respective lines.

The local authorities had analysed the company's accounts for the year to December 1922. The revenue arising in each authority's area was calculated; the total working expenses, which were equivalent to 14·05*d.* (£1.33) per car mile, were allocated pro rata to the mileage run in each area. The outcome of this as far as Chadderton was concerned was a profit of £3,839 (£87,000) representing 35·05% of the total profit, and this percentage of the purchase consideration gave Chadderton's share at £27,690 (£630,000) (Middleton's was £40,835 and Rochdale's £10,475): Chadderton's 35% share of the stores and spares cost £1226. 15*s.* 0*d.* (£28,000).

The company's rolling stock was allocated by the three tramway managers as follows: Chadderton, seven small single deck cars; Rochdale, four double deck cars; and Middleton the balance, which comprised one double deck car, one small single deck car and ten single deck combination cars. Since Middleton had decided to lease its portion of the lines to Manchester, it sold its allocation of trams to Manchester, for £100 (£2,300) each. In turn, Manchester resold the double deck car and the small single deck car (No. 31) at the same price to Rochdale and Oldham respectively.

Under the provisions of its 1925 Act, which had not at that time received the Royal Assent, Oldham agreed to purchase the Chadderton section, 1 mile 1170 yards of route, effective from 1st July 1925, at the total amount eventually apportioned to Chadderton. Through its re-sale on this date to Oldham, Chadderton probably achieved the distinction of the shortest period of ownership of a tramway in the U.K. In June 1927 Oldham received £1,633 (£42,000) from the sale of surplus ex. M.E.T. items.

A special meeting of Chadderton council had been held on the evening of Thursday, 11th June, for the purpose of passing a resolution to purchase the portion of the traction company's undertaking within the Chadderton district. This resolution was passed by the necessary two-thirds majority. Disappointment was expressed that, contrary to expectations, through services from Oldham to Middleton would not be possible on Tuesday 16th (the first day of ownership)despite the fact that the two systems would be connected by that time. The delay was mainly caused by the lack of similar connections to the Rochdale and Manchester systems and the desire of those authorities to operate the Middleton system as an entity in the meantime.

For the time being therefore, the Middleton company's system continued to operate with the same services but at reduced fares, and in the first week 10,000 extra passengers were carried. However, on 9th August, Manchester, Rochdale and Oldham took over their respective interests in the acquired lines. On this day, Manchester and Rochdale commenced to operate a joint through service via Middleton, Salford trams were extended from Rhodes (about 1¾ miles south west of Middleton), to Middleton Market Place, and the Oldham service on Middleton Road was extended to Middleton Market Place.

The company had operated a service from Rhodes through Middleton and Chadderton to the Oldham boundary, and the Oldham extension to Middleton was intended as a temporary arrangement pending through running to Rhodes. However, events decreed that the Oldham trams never operated beyond Middleton centre. The fare from Oldham to Mills Hill (the boundary of Chadderton and Middleton) was 2½*d.* (25p), with the through fare at 3½*d.* (35p). The railway bridge at Mills Hill limited operation to single deck trams and Oldham used the cars acquired indirectly from the

Middleton company, renumbered 113-120 in the Oldham fleet.

As early as September it was apparent that the Middleton service was unsatisfactory. Mr. Jackson reported that the previous evening between 5.22 and 6.0 p.m. it had been virtually impossible for anyone to board a car at the Free Trade Inn (the Oldham / Chadderton boundary). As an experiment some cars were going to run a shorter distance but this would have its effect on other services because of an overall shortage of trams. He said that he "could not put any doubtful cars, like those little Middleton ones, on the Middleton Road hill, as the risk was too great". At that time there were 110 cars available, which suggests that only two of the ex-company cars were in serviceable condition. Since the normal services required 68, and another 34 were needed for the workmen's services at night, there was an insufficient margin to allow for repairs and overhauls. Mr. Jackson was instructed to report with a view to the purchase of more trams.

The following month, a deputation attended from Chadderton to complain about the service in the district and Councillor Cheetham was able to tell them that 12 new trams were on order. Councillor Liddle, Chairman of Chadderton Council said that the tram service was "very seriously wrong in Chadderton. He personally did not know of any methods of improvement unless they abolished the 'rabbit hutches' that they were running through the district". Oldham said that the cars that they had taken over from the company had had to be repaired and re-fitted and it was essential to use every car they had. There were also problems with the overhead equipment which was inadequate for an improved service. The long stretches between loops also caused problems. Councillor Cheetham said that the matters were receiving attention and "as soon as possible we shall put down a new service, with additional loops, so that in a short time Chadderton will have a service as good as ours".

Plate 86. A general view of Hollinwood with Pilcher car 173 on the 20 route, apparently on a warm day judging by the open windows. Oldham car 18 has reversed at this point.

Further complaints about the Middleton Road service were aired in December and Mr. Jackson mentioned that a 7½ minute service was to be introduced from Market Place to Mills Hill. He had offered to put on a 10 minute service between Mills Hill and Middleton but Manchester felt that this was not warranted. Manchester, as lessee of that section, took the receipts and paid Oldham's working expenses so that any loss would fall on Manchester.

Plate 87. The Pilcher tram seen in the previous photograph has now resumed its journey to Waterhead, and has passed Oldham 7 on the same route travelling in the opposite direction to Manchester.

TROLLEYBUSES TO ASHTON

AT Ashton's invitation Oldham had attended a meeting on 12th July 1923 to discuss the substitution of trolleybuses (known at the time as trackless trams) for trams on the joint route between the two towns. Ashton, faced with the high cost of reconstructing the tracks acquired from the Oldham, Ashton & Hyde Company, considered that it would be more economic to introduce trolleybuses.

Oldham agreed with Ashton's views and passed the necessary resolution at a special meeting of the town council on 2nd January 1924, to seek the appropriate powers in the Bill being promoted in the next session of Parliament. The resolution specified operation in Oldham from the boundary in Ashton Road, thence along Ashton Road, King Street, Wellington Street, Chaucer Street, Union Street and King Street to its junction with Wellington Street. Councillor Schofield thought that Ashton Road was too narrow for running "Bulky Buses" and that "the best way to run tram cars was on tram rails". An indication of likely developments was given by Councillor Cromar who suggested that the time was not far distant when the committee would have to consider track reconstruction, the cost of which was then so great that he thought the council would reject any proposal to reconstruct the tracks leading into the outer districts. That was the primary reason for the proposed experiment with trolleybuses. He suggested that Oldham would never reconstruct the track on routes such as the circular route or to Royton and Shaw. Oldham went along with Ashton's proposal to use the Railless system.

To obtain the requisite powers it was necessary also for Ashton to promote a Bill. Oldham asked Ashton to include a clause for through running. Oldham successfully resisted pressure from the Ministry of Transport for the inclusion of a clause requiring the removal of the tram rails if requested by the Ministry. In contrast, by the subsequent Ashton-under-Lyne Corporation Act, 1924, Ashton was under such an obligation in respect of tram routes superseded by trolleybuses. Oldham accepted Ashton's invitation to visit trolleybus systems in Birmingham and Wolverhampton on 10th January 1924 and subsequently on 24th April the Oldham Committee inspected a trolleybus at the Hathershaw terminus.

The official inspection of the new system took place on Monday, 15th June 1925, when the installation was approved subject to replacing some of the poles. The trolleybus service duly commenced on Wednesday 26th August, representing the first serious reduction in the Oldham tramway route mileage, only weeks after its expansion by the extension to Middleton. For the opening ceremony the Oldham party travelled from the Town Hall to Ashton by motor bus where they were joined by the Ashton representatives and officials of various tramway authorities. The trolleybuses were then boarded and left for Oldham watched by a large number of the general public, the first one being driven (appropriately) by Alderman Oldham, Chairman of Ashton Tramways Committee. The journey to the Ashton boundary was watched with interest, and the event passed off satisfactorily apart from trolleys coming off the wires at Hathershaw where street works were underway. At the boundary the two Oldham vehicles were awaiting the Ashton cars, and the first was set in motion by Councillor Cheetham, travelling to the Star Inn and then back to Ashton. Tea was served at Ashton Town Hall. The editor of the Municipal Journal responding to the toast "The Press" said there were about 15 trolleybus systems in the country but only one of the towns could boast a tramway system and motor bus services as well. The service was operated by eight Ashton and two Oldham vehicles, numbered 1 and 2. The Oldham terminus was at the Star Inn, reached via King Street, Wellington Street, Chaucer Street and Union Street West, with the return journey via King Street and Ashton Road; the Ashton terminus was at Ashton Market. Public service commenced immediately after the official opening; there was a five minute frequency.

Trams continued to operate between Hathershaw and Summit, sharing the positive wire of the trolleybus system. Because of the poor condition of the tram track to Ashton, Oldham had used only open top cars on the route; it soon found that the road surface was equally unkind to the trolleybuses, which were solid tyred vehicles.

The Ministry of Transport was pressing for the use of aluminium wheels on the trolleybuses, which involved Oldham in discussions with the Railless Company, but eventually the Ministry dropped its insistence on immediate replacement. Approval for the system had been given only for four months but in December full authorisation without time limit was granted. Discussions took place with Ashton regarding the severe vibration problems and Ashton said that it would be fitting "cushion tyres" when the existing tyres needed replacing; Oldham decided to follow suit. The Ministry's continuing interest in the system was reflected in a further inspection on 19th March 1926 when representatives of Oldham, Ashton and Railless were required to attend.

Given the continuing complaints from residents and shopkeepers over the nuisance caused by the vibration, Oldham decided that "endeavours be made to formally dispose of the vehicles in question". In March it was decided to hold vibration tests with two other types of Railless vehicles fitted with pneumatic tyres, and with an Ashton trolleybus fitted with a new type of tyre. Finally, in April, Oldham decided to seek quotes from two firms to supply four new vehicles, taking the two existing ones in part exchange. Richard Garrett submitted a quote but Oldham decided to defer consideration of this to its meeting on 20th May. Oldham said it would be necessary for Ashton to purchase two vehicles with pneumatic tyres and thought that since Ashton would be absorbing Hurst Urban district on 1st April, 1927, it might introduce a trolleybus service since the track there was due for renewal. In this case, additional rolling stock would be required and two pneumatic tyred vehicles could be allocated to the Oldham service. Under no consideration would Oldham consent to solid tyres being used on the Oldham section. In discussion on 25th June Ashton would not agree to use a lighter type of trolleybus fitted with pneumatic tyres.

Finally, Oldham suggested to Ashton that Oldham should supply four trolleybuses with pneumatic tyres and Ashton two and that since Oldham would then be providing a disproportionate amount of the mileage run in relation to the route distances in each authority's area, Ashton should pay Oldham for the excessive mileage at 15*d.* per mile; also that this arrangement should be the subject of a five year agreement. Ashton claimed that this would provide a revenue of £4,000 a year to Oldham and a profit of £800 to £900 at Ashton's expense. Finally, Ashton claimed that the vibration with its trolleybuses was no worse than that of the Oldham buses running alongside them which had been introduced (on 2nd April) on the Hathershaw – Summit service. Needless to say the proposals were unacceptable to Ashton and so on 19th July, Oldham decided to cease operation on 5th September provided the trolleybuses had not been sold before then. Thus after a relatively short working life of a little over a year, they operated in the Oldham area for the last time on 5th September. Ashton continued to operate its portion of the route, and as late as October 1937 wanted to extend the service to the former tram terminus at Star Inn with the Oldham tram service curtailed to the same point. Oldham refused, citing inconvenience to passengers between Hathershaw and Summit caused by the need to change at Star Inn.

The trolleybuses were single deck vehicles with centre entrance built by Railless Limited and seated 36; they were 26 feet long and 7 feet 4 inches wide, and weighed 9 tons fully laden. They were powered by two English Electric DK99 motors of 35 h.p. and cost Oldham £3,315 (£80,000); equipping the line cost a further £2,148 (£52,000). In the short period of operation they ran 81,512 miles and carried 1,119,363 passengers.

A possible sale of the two vehicles fell through and in January 1927 Oldham decided to retain them for possible re-use given that improvements were being made to the condition of Ashton Road. They remained in the former tram depot in Copster Hill Road and eventually, in June, 1929 the Manager was authorised to dispose of them; they were then bought by Ashton.

Meanwhile, special attention was being given to the portion of the Middleton Electric Traction System acquired in 1925. The overhead equipment, feeders and standards in particular, were thoroughly overhauled and repaired. Triple insulation was provided because electric street lamps were being fitted to the tram standards.

On 6th April 1927, Oldham introduced a bus service between Middleton, Market Place and Shaw, Bridge Street (beyond Wren's Nest). The route included a portion of the tram route to Middleton, along Oldham Road, Middleton, from Hilton Fold Lane, and Middleton Road, Chadderton to Haigh Lane, a length of some 1,100 yards.

Middleton frequently complained to the various municipal operators about the tram services provided; in August 1928, Oldham was told about "considerable overcrowding" and poor facilities on its trams. Oldham's reaction was that a 15 minute through service was run to Middleton by arrangement with Manchester and returns indicated that this was adequate. The local traffic, Oldham said, was a matter for Manchester. At this time Manchester was reconstructing the tracks in Middleton. It was necessary during this work to change cars in Oldham Road, and Middleton alleged that insufficient time was allowed, so that passengers had to wait several minutes for the next connection. Through running in the Middleton area resumed on 8th January 1929, with the Oldham cars (and Manchester cars on the Middleton Junction route) now operating over a clockwise one-way system between Middleton Station and Middleton Market Place, inwards via Oldham Road and outwards via Townley Street.

In March 1930, a petition referred to 'discomfort and inconvenience to many residents in Middleton Road caused by the constant jarring as the tramcars pass the points and crossings'.

Plate 88. Hollinwood terminus about 1938 shows Manchester tram 979 on the part day 21 route and Oldham 24 on the 8 route to Shaw, ready to commence their respective journeys. The former depot, partly obscured by the bus, and now operated by Ferranti Limited, has had the entrances bricked up.
Photo, W. A. Camwell

Plate 89. A War time scene taken from the same spot as the previous photograph. Hoods have been fitted to the section breakers between the Manchester and Oldham systems, the trams have whitened fenders, the Manchester tram has an emergency light above and to the right of the fleet number, its trolley is being turned by a conductress, white bands have been painted on the tram standards, and the Manchester ones have lost their ornamental bases to provide scrap for war purposes.

RENEWAL OF LEASES

THE Lees lease had expired on 31st July 1924, on which day Oldham hosted a meeting with Lees, and with Royton and Crompton whose leases were due to expire on 31st December 1925, to discuss renewal terms. Oldham agreed to continue the service in Lees temporarily whilst a new agreement was negotiated. In subsequent discussions, the Districts suggested that the new leases should be on the same basic terms but with various modifications. They wished to be involved in proposed changes in stages or fares, hours of workmen's cars, the use of the tramway standards for street lighting, and most importantly they wanted a higher rent. The proposed increases were of the order of 10%, namely an annual rental for Royton of £4,022 (£97,000) (then £3,677. 11*s.* 8*d.*), Crompton £1,477 (£36,000) (then £1,293. 17*s.* 10*d.*) and Lees £418 (£10,000) (then £376. 4*s.* 6*d.*). They contended that the track and equipment had increased greatly in value because of recent increases in the cost of labour and materials, the considerable value built up in the tramways as an established service, and their value as feeders to Oldham's system, and in the development of Oldham as a shopping centre; they also referred to a "serious loss" to the three districts totalling £11,327 (£270,000) over the 21 years representing the unexpected deduction of tax from the existing rentals.

Mr. Chamberlain said that the authorities were of the opinion that the tramway traffic in their districts was the source of considerable profit to Oldham and that they wanted a price for what they regarded as the goodwill value of the lines. He agreed that a profit rent should be paid if Oldham was taking advantage of any goodwill by operating tramways in these districts; however, he contended that the goodwill had been directed towards the reduction of fares and the granting of privileges common to all users of tramways without regard to the districts in which they lived. On a comparable basis he contended that at the very least Oldham would be entitled to pay £27,621 (£670,000) annually to the Oldham ratepayers if the three districts were to receive a total of £5,917 (£143,000) as they proposed. Their proposals were equivalent to the payment of 3*d.* (30p) per car mile, without accepting any responsibility for carrying on the tramway undertaking, whereas Oldham would have to meet any deficit on the year's working.

Regarding the claim of the increased value of the track and equipment Mr. Chamberlain said that on the contrary it stood at little higher than scrap value and its life had been extended only by very heavy costs of maintenance through electric welding of the rail joints and re-equipping with new points and crossings. Although these charges might be termed renewal charges as compared with ordinary maintenance they had been borne by the undertaking.

Oldham offered three alternatives to the districts:

1. The payment of a nominal rental of £25 (£600), Oldham to maintain and renew the tramways as previously, with provision for an agreed purchase price of the track and equipment at the end of the lease.
2. Payment of a nominal rental of £25, Oldham to maintain the track and equipment but the districts to renew as required, Oldham paying a rental based on the cost of such renewal.
3. The districts to operate the tramways in their respective areas, receiving the revenue in the area concerned and pay-

Plate 90. Oldham number 11 turns into Oldham Street, Manchester, after its brief excursion into Piccadilly. *Photo, W. A. Camwell*

ing Oldham the expenses of operation. This system was the normal basis for inter-running by authorities as for example Manchester and Oldham, and Ashton and Oldham.

Mr. Chamberlain said that although the third option might entail "certain minor difficulties in working" he considered it "an excellent opportunity for the out districts to obtain close knowledge of the responsibility of tramway management, at the same time giving them the opportunity of putting in force the views they have from time to time expressed regarding the fixing of fares and stages. It would also have an effect upon the apparent readiness of the out districts in granting motor omnibus licences to outside companies".

He also stressed the possibility of changes in the form of traction in the coming years and thought that a twenty-one year lease was too long a period for Oldham to undertake. Finally, Oldham suggested that if they did not like any of the proposals they should put forward suggestions of their own.

Eventually, in April 1925 it was possible to establish Heads of Agreement for new leases as Chamberlain ended his tenure at Oldham. Despite the possibility of the trams being replaced, new twenty-one year leases were agreed with the three authorities at a yearly rental of £250 (£6,000) net of tax at 4*s.* 6*d.* (22.5p) in the £ per route mile. It was stipulated that rents would be reduced pro-rata for track reconstruction of a minimum 100 yards. The annual payments were: Royton £1,026. 0*s.* 8*d.* (£24,000), Crompton £368. 15*s.* 1*d.* (£8,800) and Lees £91. 1*s.* 10*d.* (£2,200); these amounts were only about one quarter of those originally suggested, reflecting the strength of the manager's case. Significantly, the districts shied away from operating the lines themselves.

Plate 91. A Wartime view of 131 fitted with headlamp masks seen in Oldham before descending Manchester Road. *Photo, M. Marshall*

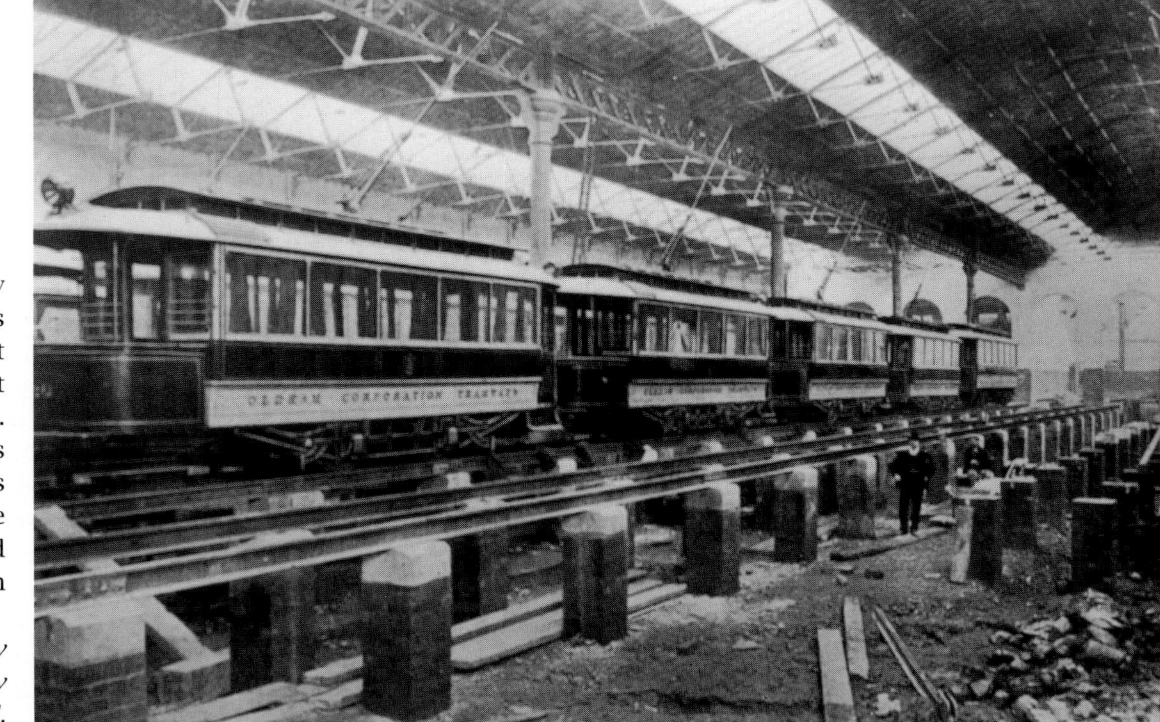

Plate 92. Newly delivered trams seen in the as yet unfinished depot at Walshaw Street. With the rails mounted on pillars the whole of the depot area served as a pit to assist in maintenance. *Light Railway and Tramway Journal.*

DISPUTE WITH ROYTON

IN September 1925, Royton appointed Arthur R. Hoare of Stephen Sellon & Partners, Consulting Engineers, London to inspect the Royton tramways and report for a fee of 50 guineas. At a meeting in November, Royton considered Hoare's report and decided to inform Oldham that the terms of the new lease were agreed and also that - as requested by Oldham - the ornamental work on tram standards could be removed when the poles were repainted. Oldham had removed the scroll work on all poles outside Royton in 1920 and 1921 because of corrosion; many pole bases had also been removed where corrosion had occurred. The Unemployment Grants Committee had contributed £1,650 (£39,000) towards the cost of painting the standards throughout the system. However, Oldham was concerned about the state of the tracks in Royton from Sheepfoot Lane (the Oldham boundary) to Royton Town Hall and in December 1925 was considering operating buses between Summit and Hathershaw. The Oldham Watch Committee intimated in January 1926 that it had no objection to the operation of double deck buses on the Hathershaw - Summit route, nor on any other tramway route within the borough.

Oldham notified Royton that the stretch of track in Royton extending from Sheepfoot Lane to Shaw Road needed relaying at an estimated cost of £10,000 (£240,000). Mr. Jackson said that three lengths on the system required renewal in the near future and they could not all be dealt with in one year; it was essential to deal with the Royton section by Spring 1927.

At its meeting on 11th March 1926 the committee was told that Royton, having obtained expert opinion, was of the opinion that it was not necessary to do the work. The Chairman expressed surprise at Royton's attitude - "any layman going over a track would know it was done. Who the expert was he did not know, but he did not attach much importance to his opinion". The Manager said the stretch was the worst length on the system. Another member expressed the view that it was an unfortunate state of things that as the authority running the trams, they were not competent judges as to whether a section of track was worn out and required replacing.

Under the terms of the lease Royton would lose rental at the rate of £250 per route mile per annum in the event of reconstruction and this clearly was a major influence in its stance. Oldham reiterated that the track "is rapidly becoming unfit for the safe running of tramway traffic" and requested Royton to reconsider its decision.

Possibly influenced by the state of the track, Oldham introduced buses between Hathershaw and Summit on 2nd April 1926 while maintaining a reduced tram service. However, apart from the morning rush period and evening workings no trams were operating beyond Royton Town Hall; this section was beyond the portion which Oldham wished to renew! Royton objected to this situation and in further discussions over proposed track renewal said that its original idea was that the tram service would be supplemented by buses: Royton would not object if every other tram had run to Summit. Oldham said that a better service was being provided, but Royton claimed that the buses were not popular. The buses were in fact running a greater mileage than the trams on the route with higher receipts per mile at 18·11*d.* (£1.86) compared with 14·56d (£1.49).

Oldham contended that the track foundations had disintegrated and to prove the point, on 15th April, excavated the road in four places about 80 yards apart; the Royton representatives present agreed that this was so. However, Royton thought that Oldham had selected the worst places and at Oldham's suggestion Royton then selected a further point for excavation. At the point in question some 300 yards further along, the road surface seemed excellent, but the underbed was found to be even worse than in the four places previously opened. Oldham claimed that Royton's reaction then was "we are going to give you a concession by allowing you to spend £10,000 on the track. What are you going to give us".

At a meeting on 30th April the Royton Committee considered the results of the inspection and the conditions found and also considered correspondence received from the consulting engineer. It was decided to ask Oldham for plans, specification, and full particulars of the proposed reconstruction in order to formulate a recommendation to the Royton council.

The committee also discussed the service of trams and buses operating on the Hathershaw-Summit route, particularly between the railway station and the boundary at Summit. It noted that:

"Notwithstanding that the representatives who

interviewed the Tramways Committee some months back were told that the bus service then proposed would be supplementary to the tram service, it was again pointed out that apart from workmen's hours, the last cars at night, and during weekends, the sole service on this route during the forenoons, and throughout the day and evening between the railway station and Summit boundary was a bus service only".

It was also reported that the Ministry of Transport had approved Oldham's plans for bus services outside the borough which had been the subject of a recent inquiry. Royton was not satisfied with the bus service and requested the restoration of the through tram service.

A meeting of the Tramways Committee on 20th May 1926 was attended by a deputation from Royton. In an extensive discussion Oldham pointed out that the state of the track was causing damage to the trams – there had been two or three broken axles in recent weeks – and the cost of maintaining the rolling stock used in Royton was higher than that of rolling stock used on any other section of the system. Royton said that whilst the condition of the concrete under the tram track was not what they had expected to find, it was intact, and Royton Council had been advised by "an engineer competent to express an opinion" that if some patching were done the track might continue to be used for the time being. Royton claimed that some damage had been done as a result of the high speed of the cars on certain lengths. Given the state of trade, Royton was anxious to avoid any loss of revenue and claimed that the track was good for two or three years. Oldham was surprised by Royton's contention that the buses were not as popular as the trams and stated that receipts per bus mile were 18·11*d.* (£1.89) compared with 14·56*d.* (£1.52) on the trams over the previous two weeks; mileages were 4,420 and 3,515 respectively. Royton countered that many used the buses through not knowing whether the trams would go further than Royton Town Hall.

After retiring, the Royton deputation returned to say that it was prepared to recommend to Royton council that the track should be reconstructed by the year end and the tram service reinstated, supplemented by a bus service as Oldham thought necessary; in addition, Royton required details of the relaying and materials to be used. Oldham couldn't agree to the conditions suggested by Royton and under the terms of the lease Oldham referred the question of the reconstruction to the Ministry of Transport. The Ministry declined to get involved and suggested that the matter should be settled by arbitration.

A further deputation from Royton on 1st July was told that if the council agreed to reconstruction, three six-wheeled Guy buses (fleet numbers 18-20) which were then being ordered would be used on the Royton section. Finally, on the 7th, Royton agreed to the reconstruction for completion by the year end on the understanding that Oldham would take off all the buses or reduce the mileage very considerably and restore the original tram service.

Figures presented at a meeting on 15th July showed that in the previous two weeks the buses had operated 12,476 miles with average receipts of 19·26*d.* (£1.97) a mile compared with 9,078 miles and 16·14*d.* (£1.65) for the trams. In the light of these figures Oldham was surprised at Royton's objections. Royton said some of the residents in Rochdale Road objected to vibrations and Oldham contended that "it was strange that the only people who were complaining to the committee were some 60, who forwarded a requisition, and who all lived within a matter of 200 yards of the terminus itself, at a point where the buses had not had time to get up speed even if the drivers so desired. One gentleman said he objected to the smell of petrol. Such an objection in the year 1926 was inexcusable".

Oldham was not prepared to accept Royton's terms regarding the buses and at this meeting decided to go ahead with the reconstruction and provide the minimum tram service stipulated in the lease, namely a 20 minute service between 6.00 a.m. and 11.00 p.m. on weekdays and Sunday afternoons, and 30 minutes on Sunday mornings. Any additional traffic requirements would be met by buses.

During these discussions Oldham had been pressing Royton to issue further licences for bus operation but was told by Royton "that in view of the understanding when the council agreed to issue licences, that the buses were to supplement the trams only and the apparent policy of the tramway committee not being in accordance therewith, the council do not see their way to grant any further licences". It was ironic that at this time the Oldham buses were housed (but not for much longer) in the former steam tram depot in Dogford Road, Royton. Eventually, on 3rd August 1926, the two authorities were able to agree Oldham's suggestions for services of buses and trams between Hathershaw and Summit, and Royton agreed to issue the extra bus licences.

The tram service was to be every 20 minutes to the Star Inn up to 2.00 p.m. Monday to Friday and noon on Saturday, increased to a 15 minute frequency on 6th September when the trolleybus service was withdrawn, with no service on Sunday before 1.00 p.m. On Monday to Friday there was to be a 15 minute through service to Hathershaw from 2.00 p.m. and on Saturday a 10 minute service from noon to 5.00 p.m. and thence at 6 minute intervals; the Sunday frequency was 10 minutes through to Hathershaw from 1.00 p.m. The bus service was to be 10 minute frequency throughout the day Monday to Saturday and on Sunday 15 minutes to 1.00 p.m. and then 10 minutes. Royton intimated that "the acceptance is without prejudice to the council's position in the matter of the vibration caused by the buses which matter is considered to be serious".

It was now possible for the reconstruction to go ahead; the section involved was from the Oldham boundary to Royton Town Hall, totalling 1,394 yards. It will be recalled that Oldham was paying an annual rental of £250 (net after tax of 4*s.* 6*d.* in the £) per mile of route, amounting to £1,026. 0*s.* 8*d.* on a route length of 4 miles 183 yards; since the length reconstructed was now owned by Oldham and not Royton the rent was reduced - by £198 (£4,800) - commencing on 20th February 1927, to a new rental of £828. 0*s.* 8*d.* (£20,000). The reconstruction cost Oldham £13,394. 14*s.* 4*d.* (£320,000) of which £8,500 (£200,000) was met by the renewals account and the balance was charged against revenue.

Plate 93. Tram 22 seen outside the former depot at Hollinwood. *Photo, M. J. O'Connor*

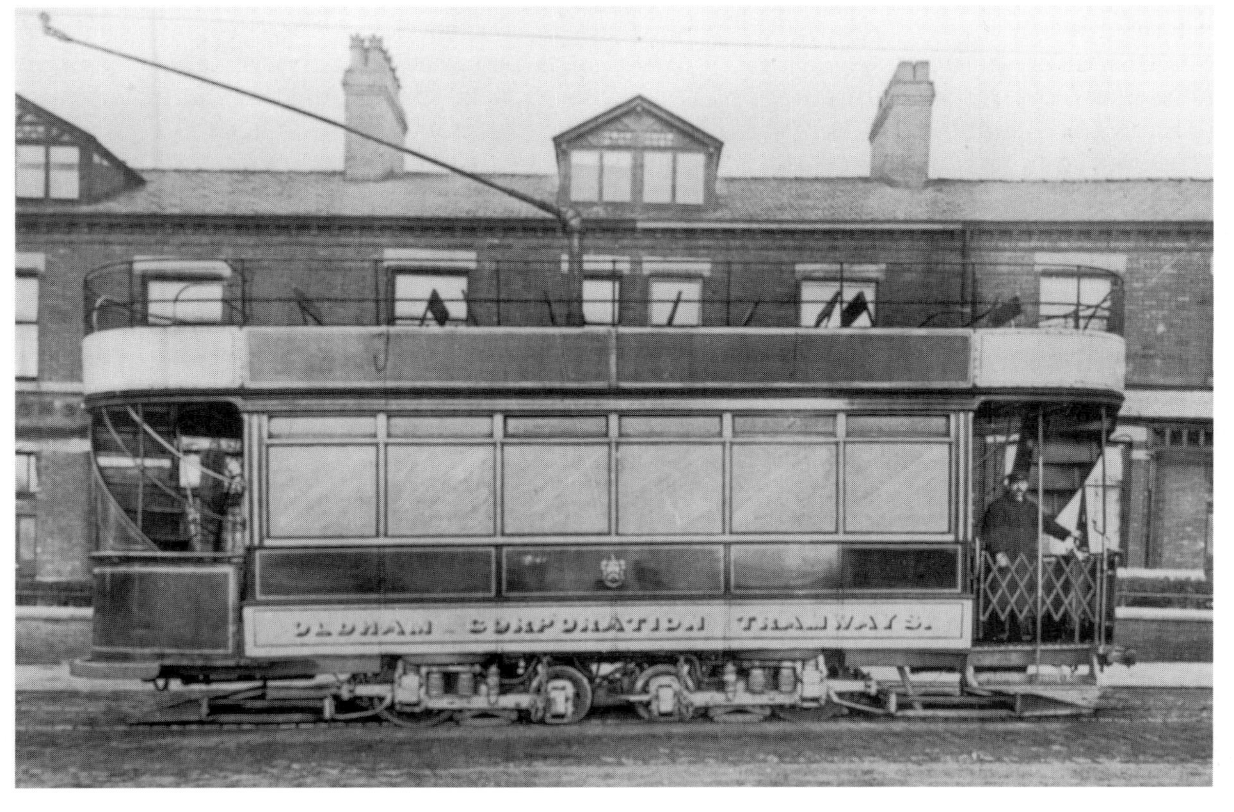

Plate 94. An early view of number 3, the only bogie double deck vehicle bought by Oldham, seen in Park Road between Retford Street and Glodwick Road.

BUSES TO LEES

IN August 1926, Mr. Jackson was able to report that Lees had agreed to the inclusion of a clause in its new lease with Oldham allowing the substitution of buses for trams on the route. Oldham had tried to amend the agreements with Royton and Crompton in similar fashion but had been turned down by both authorities.

We now move on to 22nd November when a special meeting of the Tramways Committee was called to consider the reconstruction of the Lees route track between Cross Street and the boundary, and also the financial position of the undertaking, given that a loss was being incurred as a result of a coal dispute. The outcome of this meeting was that the manager prepared a report covering reconstruction of the tramway track and also the substitution of buses for the tram service; further consideration of the financial position was deferred. Consideration of this report on 16th December resulted in a decision not to reconstruct the track and to seek Ministry of Transport approval to operate buses.

At its meeting on 12th January 1927 the council referred back the Tramways Committee's proposal for further consideration by the council in committee; this was at the request of the Tramways Committee because it was rather late in the evening and the Committee wished the matter to be discussed fully and at length. The Tramways Committee view was finally endorsed at an evening meeting on 26th January. At this meeting the Chairman of the Tramways Committee, Alderman Cheetham, said that he was anxious that the responsibility for the change in policy, which the Committee thought was now due, should be undertaken by the whole of the council and not by the eight members of the Tramways Committee.

Trolleybuses were ruled out as not being a practical proposition on Oldham's streets; there was no difficulty where they were running on macadam roads in Bardsley and Waterloo. "It would take 20 years to put the streets ready to meet the demand of the growing traffics." He said that the superiority of the trams compared with buses in coping with traffic was gradually diminishing. The Ministry of Transport was considering details submitted by a firm of bodymakers for a vehicle to seat 72 passengers, which exceeded the capacity of any of the Oldham trams.

The track in Lees Road had been given a life of 25 years and had been in use for 24 years and would not last more than a further 18 months. There was no possibility of laying a double track, which would give a more regular service. The cost of relaying was estimated at £40,390 (£960,000) whereas 14 replacing buses including two reserves would cost £26,000 (£620,000); interest and sinking fund charges on the tramway would amount to £4,036 (£96,000) a year and on the buses to £5,150 (£120,000) a year, a higher figure because of the shorter expected life of six years. Springhead Council had been pressing Oldham for travel facilities from Springhead and Grotton to Oldham and the Committee proposed that a substituting bus service should be extended from the tram terminus at County End to Station Road at Grotton.

Lees had complained to Oldham that the matter was being discussed by the Oldham council before there had been any consultation with Lees. Lees informed Oldham that there was no intention on Lees' part to allow the track to be taken up, especially in view of the agreement which existed. Subsequent negotiations with Lees secured approval for the move.

The next step was an application by Oldham to the Ministry of Transport to borrow £39,790 (£950,000) to cover the cost of buses for the Lees tram route, lifting the tracks from Glodwick Road to the Oldham boundary, and a new negative feeder in Yorkshire Street. The Ministry's reaction was that the lifting or rails was a tramway liability and not a matter for loan sanction.

Whilst these negotiations were taking place the tramway system was incurring losses because of a trade depression. To meet this situation commencing in February 1928 there was a reduction in services at certain times of the day; frequencies of 5 minutes or 7½ minutes were generally reduced to 10 minutes producing a saving of £300–£400 (£10,000) a month and curtailing the mileage by 3,400 a week. The effect on employment was to reduce the guaranteed working week of 48 hours to 45½ hours. There was criticism that these cuts were introduced at a time when Oldham had put a 72 seat bus in service (Guy, fleet number 36) competing with the trams. The bus had been bought for the Lees route and Oldham "couldn't keep it idle until it was ready for that route". Experience had shown that it could be loaded in 40 seconds and unloaded in 60.

The trams to Lees operated for the last time on 1st May, 1928 being superseded by buses the next day operating between Grotton and Market Place inwards via Yorkshire Street, St. Peter's Street and Chapel Street terminating at the top of Chapel Street; two of the vehicles had been operating to Waterhead, giving Oldham "valuable experience of the big buses". Trams continued to operate on the Hollinwood to Market Place section of the former through route. The conversion led to the abandonment of 1 mile 515 yards of route. As the road in Lees was maintained by Lancashire County Council, Lees was required to pay the county for the re-instatement of the tramway portion, at the rate of 6*s.* 0*d.* (£7.60) per square yard.

At a special meeting of Lees Council on 9th May Oldham offered a payment of £70 (£1,800) a year for 19 years, £91 a year for 15 years or a lump sum of £900 as compensation for terminating the lease. Lees opted for a lump sum, seeking £1,050 but settled for £925 (£24,000). As late as 21st November Lees decided to approach Oldham regarding the removal of the overhead wires "before there are any more accidents". Some of the track was lifted in 1931 and sold to Oldham for scrap. The bus service between Hathershaw and Summit ceased on 30th April 1928, the vehicles being required for the Lees conversion.

Whilst these negotiations had been progressing, Oldham had further expanded its bus services by instituting the following:

Shaw - Middleton 6th April 1927

Oldham - Halifax 15th April

Oldham - Greenfield 12th August

Ashton, Oldham and Rochdale 22nd February 1928

Scouthead - Gatley 8th March

Shaw - Gatley 8th March

The service between Royton Railway Station and Failsworth was amended to operate New Hey - Woodhouses on 30th July 1927. These services entailed a near doubling of the bus fleet from 22 to 42 vehicles at March 1928.

The Ashton-Rochdale service was jointly operated by Oldham, Ashton and Rochdale. "The Watcher" noted this in the Oldham Evening Chronicle two days after commencement: "the buses, which are operated by a joint arrangement between the three municipalities, seem to be fairly well patronised, and it must be a blessing for those who use them to know that they can jump from the Star Inn to Ashton Market in about a quarter of an hour, or from there to Rochdale Centre in little more than that time. The old method of getting from Oldham to Rochdale by tram, at any rate, was rather a weary process. It was a crawl from Star Inn to Summit, and then there was usually a wait there for a Rochdale tram. That excellent borough has nothing on Oldham in its tram services, and the crawl down hill into Rochdale was as slow and uneventful as the one up hill from Oldham. In the new buses the traveller gets a pleasant motor ride for a few minutes, and then has arrived. The fares, of course, are a bit up on the trams, but the improvement in the journey is well worth it".

Co-ordinated longer distance services operated jointly with other undertakings continued to be developed, including Summit–Manchester 24th September 1928, Greenfield–Manchester, Shaw–Manchester and Uppermill–Gatley (south of Manchester) on 15th May 1929. The last three represented amendments to existing services. The development of the bus services continued in the 1930s, supplemented by the conversion of tram routes as subsequently related.

Plate 95. Tram 112 rebuilt from the former number 3 with shortened body and single truck instead of bogies, and direct stairs, stands outside Walshaw Street depot.

Photo, H. B. Priestley

DRIVER TRAINING

THE indications of a gradual changeover to bus operation had prompted a debate in the council regarding Oldham training tram drivers to drive buses. The Tramways Committee was against this and was supported by the majority of the town council. The Committee's view was that it was not within their province to undertake this task. The department would be involved in financial obligations since it would take about three months training, a fully qualified tutor would have to be engaged and a number of buses, and the department had no spare buses. Although the department undertook training of tram drivers it considered the training of bus drivers as an entirely different matter. "Tram driving was a special occupation as there were no unemployed drivers available, whereas there were many motorbus drivers who could take up their duties immediately, and who possessed the necessary qualification." Opponents of the Committee's view said that men with no real experience had been taken on for bus driving whereas employees who had given every satisfaction had been turned down. The Manager's view was that any tram driver who made application as a bus driver would have the first opportunity on the buses. The Committee's attitude was that given that a change of transport was coming the men should go and learn bus driving in their spare time. "Why should the corporation teach a man his job?". On a vote 16 voted to refer the minute back and 20 were against.

Plate 96. The trams withdrawn in December 1939 were taken to Manchester for scrapping and some are here seen in the permanent way yard at Hyde Road in January 1940. From left to right they are numbers 31, 40, 34, 7, 20, 30 and 45.

Photo, E. Fielding

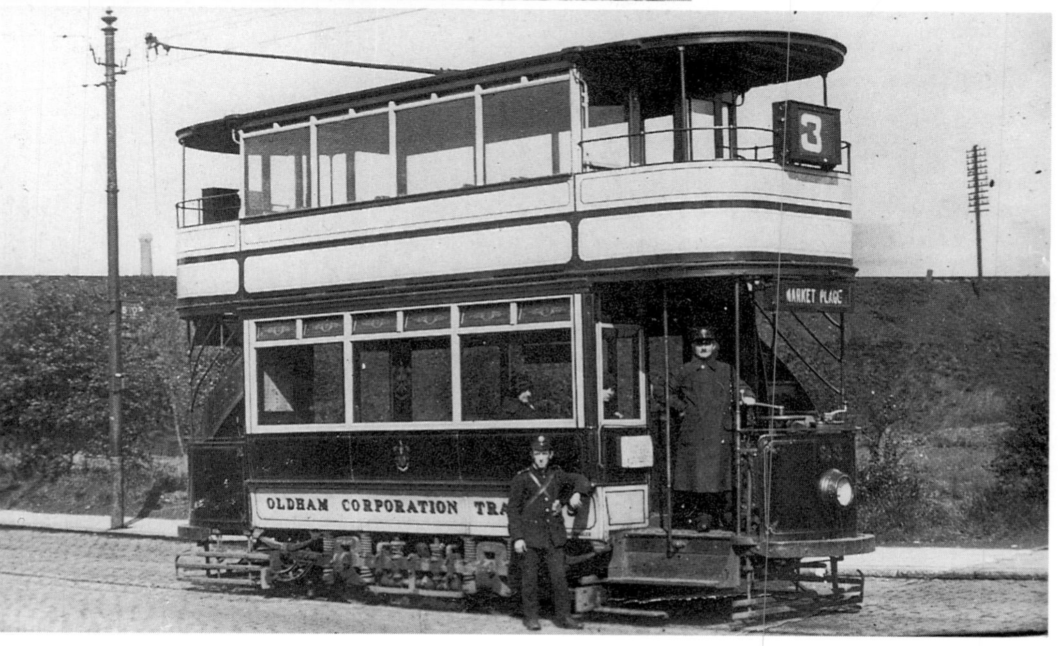

Plate 97. A specially posed view of No. 93 against the railway embankment near Mills Hill Bridge where, until late 1935, the headroom was insufficient for double deck trams. It would seem that this tram was rebuilt from the original open-topper No. 38 following the two accidents referred to in the text.

Photo, Smiths Studio.
Courtesy Mrs. R. Catterall

CONVERSION OF GRAINS BAR ROUTE

UNFORTUNATELY, the conversion of the Lees route was not to prove an isolated event. On the next day the Committee inspected the Ripponden Road track to Moorside and concluded that it was "in a very unsatisfactory condition". Because of the expense of renewal it was decided to discontinue the tram service as soon as possible in favour of buses running to Market Place via Union Street and George Street and out via Yorkshire Street. The trams operated to Grains Bar for the last time on 23rd December 1928 but the portion of route between Hollinwood and Mumps Bridge via Hollins Road continued to operate. Also the tracks from Huddersfield Road to Watersheddings were retained for traffic to the Rugby Football ground. The trams were subsequently cut back to operate between Hollinwood and Market Place via Hollins on 14th October 1929. At this time the tracks from Moorside to Grains Bar were being lifted, and the road remade, but the work was discontinued after 362 yards of single track had been removed because of the high cost of road reinstatement. The overhead was dismantled from Alva Road to Grains Bar. By June 1934 the whole of the Ripponden Road tracks had been removed.

Plate 98. Car 49 seen in its final form with six window upper saloon, upholstered seating, and truck guard, in 1932.
Photo, Geo. E. Rowland & Son

BUS GARAGE EXTENSION

THE early buses had been housed temporarily in the former steam tram depot in Dogford Road but following the purchase of land, the fleet was transferred to new premises in Henshaw Street, on 10th October 1926. The expansion of the bus operation from 17 vehicles then to 56 in January 1929 outstripped the accommodation and an extension was therefore made to the premises. The extension was opened on 13th June 1929, this day incidentally being the 80th anniversary of Oldham receiving its charter of incorporation. At that time the Oldham fleet was unchanged at 56 vehicles of which 39 were six-wheeled, and it was stated that the enlarged garage could accommodate upwards of 100 vehicles. Alderman Cheetham referred to the extent of the competition, which from a certain point of view included the Oldham Watch Committee: "who were more than ready to grant licences to all and sundry, to people who would not maintain a regular service but who were quite prepared to tap traffic during the peak hours". He considered that the department was quite successfully going through the transition period. "Had they not met outside bus competition by running their own buses then the day would not have been far distant when the last tram would have disappeared from the streets of the town. In effect their 56 buses was their last line of defence so far as their trams were concerned".

It has to be recorded however that to March 1928 there was an overall loss of £2,809 (£69,000) on the bus services, and only one year, to March 1927, had recorded a profit. In fact the buses continued to lose money, accumulating a deficit of £40,257 by March 1932; thereafter they became profitable. Whilst therefore they protected Oldham's share of the market in competition with other operators, notably North Western, the financial impact, in the shorter term at any rate, acted as a drain on the financial stability of the undertaking as a whole. For the year to March 1928 the trams carried 34,916,106 passengers with receipts of £216,185 compared with the buses' 7,081,660 passengers and receipts of £54,152. During this trading period Oldham concluded an agreement with North Western on 19th July 1927 which led to a credit of £19. 6*s.* 8*d.* in that year's accounts. This agreement continued for five years until Oldham gave notice of termination in August 1932.

Plate 99. The upper deck interior of car 49.

Photo,Geo. E. Rowland & Son

REORGANISATION IN MIDDLETON

Mr. Jackson resigned as manager in November 1929 on being appointed General Manager of Plymouth Corporation Transport. The committee had anticipated this event; on 31st October Mr. Richards, the rolling stock superintendent, attended as requested by the committee and was appointed General Manager at a salary of £650 (£16,000) rising by two annual increments of £50 to £750 in the event that Mr. Jackson was appointed at Plymouth.

Middleton was still dissatisfied with the tram services and pointed out to Chadderton that until the headroom of the railway bridge at Mills Hill was increased to allow double deck cars to run through from Oldham, it was not possible to make satisfactory arrangements. Chadderton had approved this work but progress had been delayed owing to difficulties with the railway company. The problem was that the railway could not produce the required plans since the technical staff were fully employed on schemes for which government assistance was being applied, and until the terms of agreement with the Lancashire County Council had been settled.

After protracted negotiations with Middleton aimed at improving the service to Oldham, arrangements were made to extend Salford's No. 77 tram service from Middleton to Mills Hill Bridge on a 30 minute frequency alternating with the newly introduced Manchester service, route No. 59 running into Manchester along Bury Old Road, and together providing a 15 minute service to the junction of Bury Old Road and Middleton Road in Cheetham Hill, Manchester. These service changes came into effect on 24th March 1930. Manchester was prepared to extend the service to Oldham when the railway bridge at Mills Hill had been reconstructed.

The new arrangements soon provoked further criticism from Middleton, particularly regarding the reliability of the Salford service, and in order to improve time keeping it was cut back to Middleton station about 1500 yards from Mills Hill bridge on 14th April. Problems persisted with the Salford service, whose route was rather longer than the Manchester service, compounded by roadworks, and at the end of July, Manchester took over operation of the 77 route from Salford. Meanwhile, Oldham relaid 628 yards of single track in Chadderton Road extending from Daisy Street to the Norden Street loop.

In December 1930, Middleton sent a deputation to Manchester to complain again about the services; Manchester promised to make special enquiries and use its best endeavours to meet Middleton's requirements. However, the course of events was almost immediately influenced by a proposal to widen the Prestwich portion (525 yards) of Middleton Road. Manchester as the lessee from 1st July 1929 was under an obligation to reposition the track in the event of the road being widened. Manchester did not wish to incur the expense and the timing of the roadworks was determined by a deadline imposed as a condition of receiving a government grant.

In discussions with Middleton proposing conversion to bus operation, Manchester pointed out that under the agreement to provide a 15 minute service between Manchester and Middleton and a 30 minute service between Middleton and Mills Hill, buses on the latter service would be standing for 20 minutes at Mills Hill; to avoid this a 15 minute service should operate over the Middleton - Mills Hill section as well. Such a service in addition to the Oldham tram service would be excessive, Manchester claimed, and suggested that Oldham should be required to cease running the trams from Mills Hill Bridge to Middleton except during peak periods. Middleton would not accept this and required Manchester to provide bus services to the frequencies of the existing tram services. The receipts on the Oldham trams over this section were paid to Manchester as lessee of the line from Middleton; Manchester reimbursed Oldham its working expenses, so that any loss fell on Manchester. The two Manchester tram services were duly replaced by buses on Sunday 20th March, 1932. However, trams continued to operate at peak periods between Rhodes and Middleton and this section of the former Middleton company's system was not abandoned until March 1933.

MORE BUS SERVICES

IN the years from 1929 onwards, Oldham steadily increased its bus services but these were generally to areas not covered by the tramways, namely: Uppermill Circular and Manchester and Greenfield on 15th May 1929, New Hey and Manchester on 19th May 1930, Market Place, Grains Bar and Denshaw on August 27th 1930, Uppermill and Manchester, 25th October 1931, Oldham, Market Place and Manchester (operated by Manchester) on 8th November 1931, and Derker and Chadderton, 30th April 1932. Over this period, commencing on 19th October 1930, Rochdale was converting its tramway system to bus operation; its route to Thornham (Summit in Oldham's terminology) was discontinued on 18th April 1931, being curtailed to Broad Lane. The whole system was converted over the relatively short period of two years, with the last service, the through route to Manchester, going over to buses on Sunday 13th Novembe, 1932. This closure entailed the abandonment of a portion of the former Middleton Light Railways, part of which was owned by Rochdale and part (in Middleton) leased by Manchester. On 28th August 1931, Manchester tram 420, which had entered service in April, had commenced tests of regenerative braking equipment operating on the Manchester–Oldham through service.

Smoke from a house chimney was blamed for an accident in Market Place on 13th December 1932. One tram was stationary at the Market Place stop and a second was travelling towards it on the line from Manchester Street when smoke from a chimney descended into the street. The driver of the moving tram said it was very dense and filled his eyes with what he thought was burning soot "I was temporarily blinded, and put on my brake very sharply, but before the tram stopped I felt a bump. I groped my way from the front of the tram still unable to see". The impact threw a passenger who was about to descend down the steps and he was taken to hospital. The conductor was thrown under the steps of the rear platform.

Since, as noted earlier, Manchester had converted its 59 and 77 tram services to buses on 20th March, Oldham was now the sole operator over the former Middleton Company's section from Mills Hill Bridge to Middleton Station. Manchester converted its service to Middleton to bus operation on 24th March 1935, the short route between Middleton and Middleton Junction going over to buses on 1st April. Thus Oldham was the last municipal operator to provide a tram service to Middleton which, since the takeover of the traction company in 1925, had also been served by the trams of Manchester, Salford, Rochdale and, from 19th May 1928, on the opening of a tramway linking Heywood and Middleton, by Bury also. This situation was probably unique in the United Kingdom.

In December 1930, road improvements were underway in the Market Place and planned for the Rochdale Road–West Street junction. It had been suggested that double track should be used at the latter intersection but in January 1931 the Committee decided that the existing single track should be repositioned as required by the roadworks.

At this time, Councillor Bainbridge claimed, there was a lot of lost mileage on the circular route, especially in the fine weather, which he claimed was due to there being so many loops. He particularly instanced the Ordnance Arms loop where he suggested cars often waited for one another for some time and that this was the subject of many complaints. The route was operated by four cars and he suggested that one should be taken off and the other three operated in one direction only with a starting point at Wellington Street or the Star Inn travelling anti-clockwise by Park Road and Glodwick. He suggested the public would benefit from a quicker service and the department from reduced running costs and the loops would no longer be required. The route length was 2 miles 750 yards and it was suggested that this would take 20 minutes operating on a one-way basis. Since it was regarded as one of the most profitable routes it was decided to take no action.

In October, the borough surveyor intimated that he was proposing to re-pave various tramway tracks. The reaction of the tramways department was that "as it was anticipated that certain of the tramway routes would be relinquished within the next few years" a cheaper material should be used during the interim period.

POWER COST

OVER this two year period, the Tramways Committee had been complaining about the high cost of current and initially the Electricity Committee declined to reduce the price. Mr. Richards then submitted a report showing that the cost of power to the tramways department was more than that paid by cotton mills even though the tramways was the biggest user. He also pointed out that the electricity department paid for cables to industrial users whereas those used by the tramways had been paid for by the department. Of municipal tramway operators, seventeen were paying more than Oldham whereas fifty-five were paying a lower price.

The Tramways Committee urged the Council to instruct the Electricity Committee to cut the price. This prompted the latter to offer a lower price for usage in excess of five million units a year, which was of no benefit since consumption by the tramways was less than this. There was the inducement of a further reduction if consumption increased through the use of trolleybuses. Finally in November 1932 the Electricity Committee conceded a price reduction, and in February 1933 the Finance and General Purposes Committee joined in urging the tramways to use more electricity and less motor spirit. Later that month the Electricity Committee attended the Tramways Committee meeting and the Manager was instructed to report on the possibilities of converting tram routes to trolleybus operation. Recognising the changing pattern of the department's activities the Tramways Committee became the Passenger Transport Committee in August 1933.

Plate 100. Maker's photograph of the sample single deck bogie car No. 4.

Plate 101. A first world war scene shows Driver and Conductor posing with tram No. 90.

CONVERSION OF MIDDLETON AND CHADDERTON ROAD ROUTES

DESPITE the pressure to increase electricity consumption, the Committee agreed Mr. Richards' proposals in May 1934 to abandon the tram tracks entering the Market Place from the North whilst retaining the overhead, but to introduce buses with a revision of the routes. This decision implied the conversion of the Chadderton Road and Middleton routes, and immediate steps were to be taken to complete road improvements at Market Place, West Street and Rochdale Road in connection with the conversions.

The Chadderton Road route conversion also involved the abandonment of the tram route along Higginshaw Lane and Heyside to Shaw including 1,544 yards of route in Royton and 950 yards in Crompton. There was an immediate reaction from Royton, given that the lease, and that of the Crompton lines, did not expire until 31st December 1946. Oldham had hoped to cease the rental payments on these two sections without compensation but the two authorities thought otherwise. At a joint meeting of representatives of the three bodies in Royton Town Hall on 19th July 1934, Oldham proposed payments of £1,224 (£36,000) to Royton and £720 (£21,000) to Crompton which it claimed represented about one-third of the rent and rates at the then level which would be payable in respect of the sections in question over the remaining 12 years of the lease. Royton and Crompton indicated their willingness to recommend that buses be substituted subject to payments of £3200 (£94,000) to Royton and £2000 (£59,000) to Crompton. The estimated cost of road reinstatement, at 6*s.* 0*d.* a square yard, was £2,007 for Royton and £1,386 for Crompton which, on the claimed compensation figures represented net retentions of £1,193 (£35,000) and £614 (£18,000) respectively. These figures they pointed out represented roughly one-third of the sums asked for by the councils which corresponded with the settlement made in the case of Lees which, from compensation of £925 and estimated road reinstatement costs of £610 was left with a net receipt of £315. In response, Oldham lifted its offers by roughly 50% to £1,836 for Royton and £1,086 for Crompton, representing roughly one half of the rent and rates due over the remaining twelve years.

The two councils also drew attention to the financial impact of the tramways on the two authorities. Whilst the capital expenditure on the tramways for lease purposes had originally been agreed at £52,000 for Royton and £18,350 for Crompton, the actual expenditure taking account of loans and interest over the initial 21 years had been £73,459 (£2.2m) for Royton and £26,171 (£770,000) for Crompton. The tramway rentals totalled £65,560 for Royton and £22,688 for Crompton leaving losses of £5,878 and £5,504 respectively, after taking account of a rental payment of £2,021 (£96. 4*s.* 6*d.* (£2,800) yearly) by Crompton to Royton; this represented a contribution by Crompton towards Royton's share of the cost of purchasing the steam tramway company. The first 8½ years of the current lease had resulted in a loss for Royton of £13,977 and a profit for Crompton of £3,134. The Royton loss was explained by the cost involved in acquiring the steam tramways, only a minor portion of which was funded by Oldham, and to spread the financial burden Royton had taken out loans extending beyond the 21 year period of the first lease, representing a cost in the second period of £21,237. Overall therefore Royton had a deficit of £19855 (£580,000) and Crompton one of £2,370 (£70,000). Among the points made, the two authorities stressed the cost of road reinstatement on the introduction of buses, the maintenance of which Oldham would otherwise be responsible for until 1946, and the saving in rates which would ensue from the adoption of buses.

The meeting concluded by the representatives indicating that they would report the proceedings to their respective councils. Later in the month both councils wrote to Oldham intimating that their proposals had been agreed by their respective councils. Oldham's reaction was to approach other municipal operators to obtain details of settlements in similar situations. A further special meeting of the Tramways Committee with representatives of Royton and Crompton councils took place on 6th September, this time at Shaw Town Hall. The outcome of these discussions was that the Oldham representatives decided to recommend the Council to agree the payments requested, namely £3,200 to Royton and £2,000 to Crompton on the understanding that both Royton and Crompton would undertake to continue to co-operate with Oldham in the operation of bus services in their respective areas.

On 24th May 1934, Oldham had told Manchester that it had decided to operate double-deck buses on the Middleton route when the railway bridge at Mills Hill had been widened and the headroom increased. The work began on 8th July and was completed later in the year; the headroom was improved to 17 feet 0½ inch. Oldham introduced double deck trams on this section on 19th December, anticipating that buses would take over at about the end of February. In fact, the trams did not cease until Tuesday 11th June 1935. The next day, the Manchester bus route 59 was extended to Shaw, worked jointly by Oldham and Manchester. The lines from Middleton to Mills Hill comprised 837 yards of double track and 686 yards of single track leased by Manchester from Middleton and represented the final closure of tracks authorised by the 1898 Light Railways Order. The Middleton Guardian noted the event in the following terms: "Tuesday night saw the last of electric tramcars in the Borough of Middleton. Only the Oldham Road section remained and the rickety and noisy old tramcars said farewell. They are now replaced by motor buses

"It is expected that this new system will accelerate the service. In order to conciliate those people who still regard trams as the best form of locomotion, it is up to the authorities to see the motor buses are of the latest type, that they are comfortable, and that they are punctual"

The overhead equipment on the Middleton section of this route remained in place until January 1936, when Middleton accepted a tender for its dismantlement and removal.

Although the negotiations with Royton and Crompton had been based on an assumed cost of six shillings a square yard for road reinstatement, as had applied for Lees, Oldham was required to pay Lancashire County Council immediately on abandonment only five shillings (£7.40) a square yard for reinstatement of the tramway portion of the road in Chadderton. The County Council then assumed immediate liability, the time of reconstruction being determined solely by the county. The setts were to belong to the county and when the track was removed the rails would be placed at the side of the road for collection by Oldham. The arrangements with Royton and Crompton were similar, and also at a cost of five shillings a square yard.

Also on 12th June 1935, Oldham's Chadderton Road to Shaw service was replaced by buses, operating between Chadderton (Burnley Lane) and Grains Bar. These route changes provided improved cross-town services and were accompanied by rationalisation of other bus routes. A week later Oldham accepted the tender of Grahamsleys for redundant trams and equipment.

In February 1935 it had been decided to carry out improvements at the junction of Manchester Road and Hollins Road, Hollinwood. The Tramways Committee didn't wish to reposition the track as part of the improvement and therefore decided to abandon the Hollins Road route. Fares generally were reduced on 18th August and because of the increased number of passengers some of the buses intended for the Hollins Road conversion were being used elsewhere. It was decided to purchase six more buses but the makers could not deliver for some months; after hiring two buses it was eventually possible to effect the conversion, and trams operated between Market Place and Hollinwood via Hollins Road for the last time on 21st December 1935, being replaced next day by an extension of the Grotton, Lees and Market Place bus service, thus reinstating the through route between Lees and Hollinwood which had been cut by the May 1928 conversion.

These conversions resulted in a sharp drop in the number of trams operated from 109 to 69 over the twelve months to March 1936. The total track length abandoned was 7 miles 756 yards comprising 4 miles 101 single and 3 miles 655 yards of double line. In the town centre the George Street tracks were retained but the conversions led to the abandonment of the tracks entering Market Place from the North including the link to George Street. The continuing extension of bus operation led the electrical engineer to write to the Tramways Committee stating that "the Electricity Committee views with considerable apprehension the fall in consumption of electrical energy for traction purposes". Another effect of the programme was that it was decided to adapt half of the floor space at the Wallshaw tram depot to house buses.

GARAGE DEVELOPMENT

EARLY in 1936 it was decided to centralise the tram and bus depots and workshops at the Wallshaw Street site. Accordingly, the land and buildings behind the existing Wallshaw Street depot were purchased; these comprised 16,165 square yards, the former site of Wallshaw Mill for £4,500, the land and premises of Joseph Gartside & Company for £2,750 and premises occupied by Austin & Company (Oldham) Limited for £3,650. Ferranti Limited were interested in purchasing the facilities at Hollinwood and the Committee agreed to sell for £8,000 with possession when possible but not within 12 months. After negotiation Oldham accepted Ferranti's offer of £6,250 (£180,000). The Borough Engineer and Surveyor drew up plans for the new central garage and offices which were estimated to cost £102,000 (£2.9m). In August, the Ministry of Transport gave approval to Oldham borrowing £129,150 (£3.7m) to cover all aspects of the Wallshaw development.

Reflecting the rearmament programme then getting underway, the director of Naval Contracts asked Oldham for a transfer of the Hollinwood works as soon as possible so that Ferranti could extend its facilities to meet the Admiralty's requirements. Because of a claim for loss of light arising from the new bus garage development, Oldham also purchased 2,705 square yards and 443 square yards with buildings in Gordon Street for £4,000 from Robert Scott Limited; these buildings formed part of Paradise Mill. Bad weather during the winter delayed the construction of the garage which had been scheduled for completion by 30th April. Oldham was anxious to release the Hollinwood workshops to Ferranti as soon as possible, and hoped to use part of the new facilities by the end of May, before completion, following which it would take two months to vacate the Hollinwood premises. At this time representatives of the transport press were invited to see the progress on the new garage. The Passenger Transport Journal in its issue of May 14th 1937 commented "...we were inclined to look upon Oldham as merely one of the highly industrialised townships in Lancashire, rather drab and dreary in appearance, and offering no particular interest in the way of transport organisation. We were quickly undeceived, at any rate in regard to the latter circumstance".

There then followed a reference to the modernisation of the original offices which had been rebuilt at a cost of over £7,000 (£190,000), and a review of the facilities which had been provided. At the time of the visit the new garage was basically a shell without any clear floor space, because of the continuing work. It was thought to be one of the largest garages of its kind in the country with, probably the largest single span, of 198 feet. On completion it was to house the existing fleet of 130 buses, and the 30 double deck buses then on order, and ultimately a total of 250. The Hollinwood premises were finally vacated at noon on Saturday 7th August, and Ferranti was informed. The new garage was officially opened on 23rd May 1938. The former garage at Henshaw Street was now no longer required and it was agreed to sell it for £4,300 (£120,000). The Ministry originally banned the sale unless Oldham repaid the existing debt on it before the sale but eventually relented on condition that the proceeds were used to repay debt with the balance over five years. However, the sale was not completed until 31st December.

Plate 102. Two different liveries are displayed in this three car line-up. *Dr. Hugh Nicol.*

CONVERSION OF SUMMIT ROUTE

NEGOTIATIONS took place with Royton early in 1937 over Oldham's proposal to convert the Hathershaw – Summit route. The length which would be abandoned in Royton comprised Oldham Road and Rochdale Road from Shaw Road to the boundary with Rochdale, a total of 1 mile 1,316 yards of route of which the first 648 yards was Oldham's property being part of the reconstructed portion and on which no rent was payable, as previously noted. The rental on the remainder at £250 net of tax per mile per year, together with the rates on the whole portion, entailed an annual payment of £472. 10*s.* 1*d.*

At a joint meeting at Royton Town Hall on 23rd February, Royton intimated that it was prepared to recommend the council to abandon the track subject to compensation for nine years rent and rates from 31st December 1937, the unexpired portion of the lease, less 10%, amounting to £3827. 5*s.* 8*d.* (£110,000). Oldham accepted the terms and said that it would not be able to convert the route before that date; Royton intimated that in the event of earlier conversion, it would not require any extra payment. In fact the conversion took place on 7th November with the service extended to Rochdale thus restoring a facility which had been discontinued some 20 years earlier; on the same date buses also replaced trams on the circular route. These latest conversions led to a further sharp reduction in the tram car fleet from 68 to 44 vehicles over the year to March 1938.

The Hathershaw–Summit route was 4 miles 931 yards long but a portion of the tracks involved was still used by the service from Hollinwood via Featherstall Road to Shaw. The conversion of the circular route involved the abandonment of the tracks in Park Road, Glodwick Road, the remaining portion of Lees Road and Union Street; Union Street West, Crossbank Street and George Street were also abandoned at this time. A total of 6 miles 979 yards of track, comprising 3 miles 57 yards of single and 3 miles 922 yards of double was abandoned.

Plate 103. Mills Hill, the limit until 19th December 1934 for double deck trams operating on route 3.

Oldham and Rochdale Corporation Passenger Transport Departments.

NOTICE

The HATHERSHAW-SUMMIT TRAMCAR SERVICE will be DISCONTINUED after completing the Daily Schedule on Saturday, November 6th, 1937.

On Sunday, November 7th, 1937, a MOTOR OMNIBUS SERVICE will be introduced, and will operate between HATHERSHAW, SUMMIT and ROCHDALE (Town Centre)

DESTINATION INDICATOR :-- HATHERSHAW AND ROCHDALE (LOCAL SERVICE) NO. 9.
HATHERSHAW AND SUMMIT (,, ,,) LETTER M.

END OF THE TRAMS

THERE were now only two routes remaining, namely from Hollinwood to Shaw (Wren's Nest) via Royton, and the route from Hollinwood to Waterhead which also carried the through trams from Manchester. In May 1939, Oldham approached both Royton and Crompton to agree terms for replacing the trams on the Shaw Road route. Royton and Crompton met together at the Royton Town Hall on 16th May and decided to recommend the respective councils to approve the conversion subject to the payment of seven years rent and rates in each instance, this being the period of lease remaining from 31st December 1939. Oldham countered with an offer of 85% of these figures but settled for 90% as had applied to the 1937 conversion on the Summit route. The payments were £2,561. 8*s.* 5*d.* (£70,000) to Royton and £2,011. 11*s.* 10*d.* (£55,500) to Crompton. The route lengths were 1 mile 47 yards owned by Royton (Shaw Road), 1646 yards in Crompton (Milnrow Road and Manchester Road), Oldham's reconstructed track in Royton, stated as 752 yards, although by deduction of the Summit conversion figure, the length would be 746 yards, and Featherstall Roads.

World War II had started on 3rd September 1939, and in response to a request from the Ministry of Transport for the reduction or cancellation of contracts, Oldham reaffirmed its policy to scrap all the remaining trams in a resolution on 27th September and said that a recent contract for 47 buses could not be cancelled. Oldham's application to borrow £82,673 (£2.2m) for the buses was at that time being reviewed by the Ministry.

Oldham said that the determination of leases was subject to delivery of the vehicles required by the end of November and also to road service licences being granted by the Traffic Commissioners. Application was also made to the Ministry to borrow the sums payable to Royton and Crompton. The necessary approvals were forthcoming, the buses duly arrived, and took over on the Shaw route on Sunday 3rd December 1939. Anticipating complete abandonment, Oldham had accepted a tender from A. Devey & Co. in July for the 44 trams then remaining. The December conversion resulted in 17 of these becoming surplus, but they were scrapped at Manchester's Hyde Road works.

In the case of the abandonments in Royton and Crompton, Lancashire County Council had undertaken, as in the case of Chadderton, to remove the rails and reconstruct the roadway on payment of 5*s.* per square yard of the area involved, the rails to be removed from site by the district concerned. Under this arrangement the amounts involved for Royton were £1,754 (Heyside) £2,626. 0*s.* 5*d.* for the Summit route and £2,138 for the final conversion. At the outbreak of war some of the tracks in Chadderton, Heyside and on the Summit route had not been lifted, nor of course had those on the final conversion. The Government was anxious for disused tram rails to be lifted to provide scrap for war purposes and offered £6 (£130) a ton. Lancashire County Council asked authorities to remove the rails, reinstating the road in strips rather than full reconstruction, and to refund the difference compared with the pre-war price of some £2. 10*s.* 0*d.* per ton to the county towards the cost of eventual road reconstruction in the tramway area. Oldham agreed to this request. In January, 1940 Royton agreed to sell twelve section insulators from the Shaw Road route to Oldham at the scrap value of £2. 15*s.* 0*d.* (£65) each and asked Oldham to dismantle them.

Trams continued to operate between Hollinwood and Waterhead throughout the war along with the through service from Manchester. Manchester had continued with its conversion of the tramway system with the aim of complete bus operation by 1940–41. It had been progressively reducing the tram services on Oldham Road through the 1930s. When Manchester introduced route numbers in 1914, they had been numbered clockwise from Bury New Road; No. 20 was allotted to the through service from Manchester to Waterhead and 21 to the Manchester–Hollinwood service. On 16th February 1931, route 23 operating from Chorlton, a southern suburb, to Newton Heath on Oldham Road had been extended to Hollinwood; at the same time the 21 service was reduced to part day operation. The 23 tram gave way to the 82 bus on 2nd July 1939 but following Manchester practice the buses were initially supplemented by trams at the peak period. They were probably still running on this basis when the war started. In order to save diesel fuel, tram services were augmented and bus services curtailed where possible. Thus, on 27th May 1940, the 23 route once again operated throughout the day, being supplemented by buses at the peak periods. The 21 service was also in evidence. In fact, more trams seem to have been operating on this service during the war than previously, for it was not uncommon to see the route number indication provided by a number 51 stencil plate inserted upside down, the 51 route by that time having given way to buses. Both the 20 and 21 services were extended from Stevenson Square to Piccadilly again, probably on 4th November 1940, when Manchester added to the trolleybuses using the Square by the introduction of a service to Harpurhey.

Manchester suffered severe air raids on the nights of 22nd and 23rd December, in the course of which a landmine caused a large crater in Oldham Road, near Linacre Street. The Lancashire Constabulary wrote to Manchester in the following terms on 15th January 1941: "As a result of the bombing in the City of Manchester on the night of 22nd and 23rd December last, I understand that tramcars are prevented from running into Manchester beyond Linacre Street, Miles Platting, and are also unable to return to the depot at Cheetham Hill Road, necessitating the parking of tramcars on the main road on the Failsworth side of Linacre Street.

"Between the hours of 11 p.m. and 5 a.m. six tramcars are usually left parked on the main road at Failsworth, and when these cars were first left on the main road it was observed that as many as three were parked together at the Failsworth - Oldham boundary, and bearing in mind the possibility of an air attack in that area, it was suggested to your local Inspector that the risk of obstruction to the essential services would be minimised if the tramcars were parked some considerable distance from each other to which he agreed and gave an assurance that this would be done.

"It is observed however, notwithstanding this assurance, that tramcars are still parked together opposite the works of Messrs. Ferranti Ltd, near to the Failsworth–Oldham boundary, and as I understand it will be another two or three weeks before normal conditions are resumed, I would be grateful for your co-operation in this matter."

Under redevelopment, Linacre Street is now the part of (an extended) New Allen Street abutting Oldham Road. The superintendent was clearly not familiar with the Manchester tramways for the depot he referred to as Cheetham Hill Road - actually Queen's Road - had closed to trams in March 1938. The outcome of this complaint was that the six Manchester trams involved were subsequently housed in Wallshaw depot until the through running could recommence. Mr. Richards died in October 1943, after a short illness, and was succeeded in April 1944, by Cyril Paige, the manager at Bury.

The through service was discontinued for a period from 4th April 1944, following an instruction from the Regional Transport Commissioner to reduce tram services by 20%. As the war approached its end conditions began to ease, so much so that on 12th February 1945, Manchester's 23 route reverted to part day operation only, the last tram running a year later on 4th May 1946.

Following the end of the war the Oldham electricity committee proposed that trolleybuses should be substituted for the trams on the Waterhead–Manchester route, at a meeting on 19th September 1945. However, the department accepted the General Manager's report that it was not the time to consider trolleybuses favourably and that the matter should be deferred on "such terms as would enable the matter to receive further consideration at a more favourable time".

In the following month, the Minister of War Transport agreed to replacement of the trams by buses and the Manager pressed for an early allocation of Leyland chassis stressing the "urgent necessity for substituting omnibuses for the existing tramway system". Fourteen were required; orders for bodies were said to be proceeding satisfactorily. In May 1946 Mr. Paige reported that because of material shortages the new buses to replace the trams would not be delivered as early as expected. Therefore, it would not be possible to replace the trams until about 1st July. This in fact proved to be optimistic.

The through route - of which 4 miles 96 yards was in Oldham - finally ceased on 3rd August 1946, buses taking over the next day. Manchester continued to operate short workings to Hollinwood, which finally ceased on 28th December.

The last Oldham tram was No. 4, an open balcony car which had been decorated with coloured pennants and illuminated five point stars at each end. The Oldham Standard reported the event in the following terms: "Oldham's 46-years-old tram service passed out of existence for ever on Saturday night in a blaze of light when a brilliantly illuminated tram followed behind the final passenger car over the town's only remaining tramlines from Waterhead to Hollinwood.

"True to his promise the Mayor in silk hat and Chain of Office drove "Light Princess" all the way from the Wallshaw Street depot to Waterhead and then to Hollinwood and back, bringing the old stager to rest in the tram shed within twenty minutes of midnight.

"Waterhead gave as animated a demonstration as Mumps and happy crowds continued to cheer the car on its return to town. At the Town Hall and on the elevation by the War Memorial multitudes continued the symphony of cheering. In the Market Place, Manchester Street, Werneth and down the stretch to Hollinwood, all had their welcomes.

"During the last lap home the tram was often slowed down by people dashing in front to place coins, pins and other articles on the lines, to be flattened out as souvenirs of this historic event in Oldham's transport history."

The passengers were civic dignitaries and in the depot the Mayor was presented with a brightly burnished tram gong mounted on wood. The Minister of Fuel and Power had originally objected to the running of an illuminated tram but approval was forthcoming after he was contacted by Oldham's M.P. A "lavishly decorated tram" had been run between two and five in the afternoon and from six until nine in the evening, and was presumably No. 4 without the illuminations.

The tram poles and section boxes were transferred to the street lighting department free of charge. It was decided to seek tenders for the trams and various items of equipment. The first committee meeting following the abandonment did not take place until 18th September when it was agreed that some equipment should be sold to A. Robinson and Company, Llandudno and Colwyn Bay Electric Railway Limited and Leicester City Transport. No offers had been received for the trams and it was suggested that they should be broken up and sold for scrap. However, the committee left the Chairman and deputy Chairman to deal with this matter and they were able to report on 20th November that tenders had been accepted for six trams from the Gateshead and District Tramway Company Limited and for twenty bodies from Middleton Tower Estate Limited. The trams purchased by the Gateshead Company operated there until April 1951.

Plate 104. The last tram on 3rd August 1946.

APPENDIX 1 - ROLLING STOCK

As mentioned in the text the first four trams were of different types to assist in evaluating the most appropriate for the system.

The following abbreviations are used in this section.

Brill - J. G. Brill Company, Philadelphia, U.S.A.

Brush - Brush Electrical Engineering Company Limited, Loughborough.

DK - Dick, Kerr & Company Limited, Preston.

EE - English Electric Company Limited, Preston.

ERTCW - Electric Railway & Tramway Carriage Works Limited, Preston.

MV - G.C. Milnes, Voss & Company Limited, Birkenhead.

Siemens - Siemens Brothers Dynamo Works Limited, Stafford.

UEC - United Electric Car Company Limited, Preston.

1. Single Deck five window saloon built by ERTCW and delivered late November 1900.

Seating: Longitudinal facing inwards for 28 persons; this was later quoted as 30.

Truck: Brill 21E 6' wheel base with 2 x 25 h.p. motors.

Dimensions: Length over corner posts 20', length over dashes 28', length over fenders 29'. Height: rail to trolley plank 10'11", height inside saloon 7'8½".

Withdrawn - 1927/28.

2. Double deck open top with three window saloon built by ERTCW and delivered late November 1900. It had reversed stairs. It was probably to the manufacturer's standard design, in which case seating would be 22 in the saloon and 34 on top.

Truck: Brill 21E 6' wheel base with 2 x 25 h.p. motors.

Dimensions: Length over corner posts 16', length over dashes 26'6", length over fenders 27'6". Height: rail to trolley plank 9'9½", height inside saloon 6'9".

Later, it was fitted with a balcony top cover and presumably direct stairs. DK. K3 Form B controls fitted 1920/21 Withdrawn 1935/36.

3. Double deck open top with six window saloon built by ERTCW and delivered late November 1900.

Seating: 68, believed to comprise 26 on longitudinal seats in the saloon and 42 on top.

Truck: 2 x Brill 22E with 25 h.p. motors but re-equipped with 40 h.p. motors in 1908.

In February 1915, the body was in use at Glodwick yard as a cabin for the platelayers; the bogies were sold to Blackpool Corporation Tramways. The body was used in 1920 in the construction of a replacement car No. 112, but shortened from six to five windows. As No. 3 it had reversed stairs, but was fitted with direct stairs when rebuilt. Four more cars of this type were ordered in August 1901, but the order was cancelled in June 1902.

4. Single deck six window saloon built by ERTCW and delivered late November 1900.

Seating: Longitudinal for 36 persons, later stated as 38.

Dimensions: Length over corner posts 26', length over dashes 34', length over fenders 35'. Height inside saloon 7'9".

Truck: 2 x Brill 27G, 4' wheel base; overall wheel base 18'6".

Electrical Equipment: originally 2 x 25 h.p. motors but re-equipped with 4 x DK 25A 25 h.p. motors in 1908. The total cost of upgrading this car and No. 3 was £713. 16*s.* 0*d.* (£31,000).

It was sold to Rotherham Corporation tramways early in 1916.

5-16. Built by ERTCW and generally similar to number 4 but, on the advice of Hewitt & Rhodes, Oldham's consulting electrical engineers, and presumably reflecting experience with the operation of that car, were fitted with 4 x DK 25A 25 h.p. motors; controllers were DBI Form D. They were delivered in the early months of 1902. Guards were fitted in the space between the bogies in 1905.

In October 1902, following a visit to Liverpool, it was decided to convert car No. 13 into a double deck vehicle by equipping it with an adaptation of the Bellamy top cover which had been seen on some of the trams in Liverpool. The Bellamy cover was rectangular in shape covering the upper deck portion corresponding to the lower saloon. This conversion entailed the removal of the clerestory and the provision of straight staircases ascending inwards from the platform thus curtailing the seating capacity of the longitudinal seats in the lower saloon. The conversion increased seating capacity from 38 to 72 - 32 in the lower saloon and 40 in the upper on 20 x 2 reversible seats. Height from rail to trolley plank was 15'6". It was available for service in its new form on 25th September 1903. Originally, the top cover was open at the sides, but was enclosed in December 1910.

The other cars in the series remained as single

deck vehicles. In November 1910 one was modified to cater for smokers, possibly by adding a partition, and it was decided to make similar alterations to a further six.

In February 1916, it was decided to sell the eleven single deck cars and also No. 4. Rotherham decided to purchase one and was given a two months option on the remainder, which it duly exercised in April. The cars had cost Oldham £950 (£45,000) each comprising £675 basic plus £60 for air brakes plus £215 for additional motors. The total cost was therefore £11,400 (£540,000) and at the time of disposal £10,136. 9*s.* 6*d.* (£480,000) had been paid to the sinking fund, leaving a balance of £1,263. 10*s.* 6*d.* (£60,000). The proceeds of this sale were £5,180 (£240,000) (£431. 13*s.* 4*d.* each) enabling £3,916. 9*s.* 6*d.* (£180,000) to be transferred to the reserve fund (renewals account) after crediting £1,263. 10*s.* 6*d.* to the Sinking Fund.

No. 13 was withdrawn in 1923/24; its seating capacity had been restated at 70 in the 1920s.

17-26. These single deck saloon cars, built by ERTCW, were ordered in August 1901 and delivered during 1902; they were generally similar to No. 1.

Withdrawn	
1917/18	17,18, 20 and 24. A saloon body was sold in April 1917.
1921/22	19 or 22
1923/24	22 or 19
1925/26	23, 26
1926/27	21
1928/29	25

27-80. Double deck single truck open top cars built by ERTCW but unlike No. 2, they had a short canopy and direct stairs.

Seating: 20 in the saloon and 28 on top comprising 2 x 3 at the ends, 2 x 1 at the sides of the trolley mast and 10 x 2.

Truck: Brill 21E 5'6" wheel base with 2 x 25 h.p. motors.

Dimensions: Length over corner posts 14'6", length over dashes 24'6", length over fenders 26'. Height: rail to trolley plank 9'9½", height inside saloon 6'9".

Nos. 27-42 were ordered in August 1901. No. 38 was the first to be delivered and was inspected on 5th December. It was fitted experimentally with a Tidswell lifeguard. Oldham decided to fit all trams with this apparatus and to order a further 25 cars. The remaining 13 were ordered in August 1902. The first 12 were in service by June 1902 and the balance by June 1903.

Commencing in August 1903 and extending until 1922 most of the cars were fitted with top covers; however, six cars, 50, 52, 55, 68, 70 and 80 were withdrawn in original open top condition; it is possible also that No. 33 which had been fitted with a top cover in 1904 reverted to original open top condition. A further five cars - 43, 47, 56, 57 and 74 - remained open top but had their upper decks extended to full car length, one in 1924/25 and four in 1925/26, with seating increased from 48 to 60. No. 43 and 47 were subsequently reduced to single deck trams in 1932/3 and 1934/5 with seating for 26 and 25 respectively to replace withdrawn cars on the Middleton route; 43 was fitted with a platform vestibule.

The seating capacity of cars fitted with Bellamy type top covers was increased from 48 to 50 because the removal of the trolley post enabled the two single seats to be replaced by double. Cars so treated were 76DK, August 1903, 13 DK September 1903, 70 MV February 1904, 58 Oldham design April 1904, 33 MV May 1904, 27-32 Oldham design November 1904, 34-36 Oldham design with Magrini fittings November 1905. Two more cars - 75 and possibly 73 - were given top covers in the year to March 1907.

Subsequently, balcony type top covers were fitted with top deck extended to full car length, with three, 77, 63 and 78, completed by March 1910. The first of these (probably 77) was inspected on 2nd December 1909; three more followed shortly afterwards. These cars then seated 56. More top covers were bought in 1912. In 1916 and 1917 at least 10 cars, including No. 66, were fitted with top covers by English Electric at Preston, with seating capacity increased to 58. By March 1919 only 17 cars remained in original open top condition.

No. 45 was rebuilt to open balcony enclosed platform condition in the year to March 1921 and then seated 54; 34 was further rebuilt to this state in the following year, when both cars were stated to seat 52. No. 40 was rebuilt from open top state to an all enclosed car seating 56 and was inspected on 4th August 1921; it was re-equipped with a Brill 21E longer wheelbase truck, DK 40hp motors and DK3 controllers. No. 54 was similarly treated in the next few months, followed a year or so later by 49 which was later stated to seat 58. No. 49. was further modernised in June 1932 when it was fitted with transverse upholstered seating in both lower and upper saloons; in its final form the three lower saloon windows each side had been modified to five, the central one being similar to the original; these were matched in the upper saloon by six equal sized windows. In this form the seating was 53. It was also fitted with a truck guard but this was later removed to facilitate maintenance and also because of corrosion.

As recorded earlier, No. 38 was involved in accidents in Crompton in June 1910 and in Salem Brow in December 1912 and is believed to have been renumbered 93; the evidence to support this suggestion is that at that time No. 92 (incidentally in collision with No. 38 in Salem Brow) was the highest numbered car in the fleet, the water car was numbered 38 about this time, and figures quoted during the war indicate that 80 cars were fitted with Dick Kerr equipment. Finally, a photograph of No. 93 in open balcony state confirms that the lower saloon was identical to those of this batch of open top cars.

Withdrawn

1922/23 27
1925/26 32
1926/27 28,52
1927/28 33,36
1929/30 55
May 1930 76
July 1930 35, 50, 68, 70, 80
1935/36 43, 47, 56, 57, 74 (it will be recalled that 43 and 47 had been reduced to single deck for the Middleton route. 56, 57 and 74 were the last open top trams in operation. Oldham had said in December 1933 that they "only operate in special circumstances".
37, 39, 42, 51, 58, 59, 61, 62, 64, 67, 71, 77
Nov. 1936 93 (ex. 38)
Dec. 1937 44, 46, 48, 60, 63, 65, 66, 69, 72, 73, 79
Dec. 1939 29, 30, 31, 34, 40, 41, 45, 49, 53, 54, 75, 78

81-92. Double deck top covered balcony cars built by UEC and delivered between June and September 1911. A trial trip was made on 20th June from Hollinwood depot to Waterhead and Moorside, returning via Union Street and Hollins Road.

Seating: 58 believed to comprise 22 in the lower saloon and 36 on the upper deck.

Equipment: Preston Flexible Truck with 2 x 48hp Siemens Motors, Siemens controllers, Westinghouse slipper brakes, and Cummins auto-sanders.

Dimensions: Length over corner posts 16'. Three window saloon with air scoops, upper saloon three windows with no quarter lights.

Problems were experienced with the motors and in January 1917 the controllers were altered with some reduction in speed to cure the problem. However, the controllers seem to have been unsatisfactory and they were replaced by DK K3 Form B controllers commencing with car 83 in 1920/21.

Cars of this class were operating to Manchester shortly after delivery. As originally built the destination indicator was fitted in the upper deck railings but was resited to a position over the driver when the original location was required for the introduction of route numbers.

Withdrawn

1936/37 81, 82, 83, 84, 85, 88, 90, 91
Dec. 1937 86, 87, 89, 92

94-99. Double deck top covered balcony cars. Ordered from UEC late in 1913, and similar to the previous batch.

Seating: 58 believed to comprise 22 in the lower saloon and 36 on the upper deck.

Equipment: Preston Flexible Truck with 2 x 48hp Siemens Motors; Siemens controllers.

In 1920/21 No. 94 was fitted with DK30 motors and K3 Form B controllers; it was also equipped with Spencer slipper brakes.

Withdrawn

1935/36 99
Dec. 1937 95, 96, 97, 98
Dec. 1939 94

100-111. In April 1914 Oldham decided to obtain tenders for a further 12 cars, six for immediate delivery. They were supplied by UEC and the first six appear to have been completed by October; the company then asked Oldham's permission to construct the second six "to provide work". Oldham was agreeable provided the company would store the cars until required. Seating capacity was 58 and the cars were similar to those of the previous batch.

Withdrawn

1936/37 100, 101, 103, 106, 107, 108, 110
Dec. 1937 102, 104, 105, 109, 111

4-12, 14-16. On 1st May 1919 it was decided to invite tenders for 12 new cars, the first since the war. They were ordered the following month from English Electric; the Committee had also visited Brush's factory. Two lower saloons were delivered on 11th June 1920 and two upper decks on the next day; all 12 trucks had already been received. A trial run was held on the first to be assembled and painted – on 24th June – and they were all in service two months later. They were the first vehicles in the fleet to have open balconies but vestibuled platforms; they took the numbers of the bogie single deck vehicles which had been sold to Rotherham during the war. The seating capacity was 58 comprising 22 in the lower saloon and 36 on the upper deck. Upper and lower saloons had three windows each side with quarter lights. Cars of this series were operating to Manchester in 1922.

Equipment: Brill 21E trucks 7' wheel base.

Withdrawn

Dec. 1939 7

Aug. 1946 4-6, 8-12, 14-16

112. This car was built by Oldham in 1920, utilising the body of car No. 3 which had been used at Glodwick Road as a platelayers hut since February 1915. Originally a six window saloon reversed stair car, in its reconstructed form the body had five windows and was fitted with normal direct stairs. It was constructed as a balcony top covered car seating 58. The upper saloon had four windows each side fitted with quarterlights as was the lower saloon.

Equipment Brill 21E truck, DK30 motors and K3 Form B controllers.

Withdrawn

Dec. 1939

17-20, 22, 24. These cars were ordered from English Electric in August 1923 at a cost of £16,490. 4*s.* 0*d.* *(£400,000)* and were the first fully enclosed cars supplied to Oldham. In connection with the purchase the Unemployment Grants Committee agreed to pay half of the interest on a loan not exceeding £10,686 for fifteen years. It was reported in December 1923 that the Ministry of Transport had held up construction since October because it objected to trap doors over the stairs and required vestibules fitting instead. The trap door was intended to close off the stairs at the driver's end of the car. The Ministry eventually relented, and the first car was delivered in July 1924 and the remainder by March 1925. The cars took the numbers of the six single deck single truck cars which had been withdrawn by then. The lower saloon had three windows with corresponding windows on the upper deck, both being fitted with quarterlights and the lower saloon with air scoops.

Seating: 64 comprising 22 in the lower saloon and 42 upstairs.

Equipment: Brill 21E trucks 7'6" wheel base. The Ministry of Transport insisted that side guards should be fitted to both sides at both ends of these cars. No. 42 was fitted with roller bearings.

Withdrawn

Dec. 1939 19, 20

Aug. 1946 The remainder. 17, 18 and 24 were sold to the Gateshead and District Tramways Company, a BET subsidiary, becoming respectively 72, 71 and 35. They were finally withdrawn in March 1951.

113-120. These were the former Middleton Electric Traction Company cars acquired by Oldham following the purchase of the company by the various local authorities. No. 31, purchased from Manchester, arrived on 29th June 1925.

The cars were built as trailers for the BET subsidiary the Oldham, Ashton and Hyde Electric Tramway Limited and were transferred to the Middleton company about December 1902. Their original fleet numbers were 27-34 which were retained on transfer to Middleton.

The cars were built by Brush with a probable length of 27' overall and 18' for the saloon. Seating capacity was 26 inside the saloon and 1 outside at each end but Oldham regarded the capacity as 26 in total.

Equipment: Originally the cars had Peckham trucks but these were replaced by Brush AA trucks on cars 28 and 34 in 1909; the Middleton company equipped the cars with 2 x 25 h.p. DK 25A motors and DK DB1 controllers. Oldham replaced the Peckham trucks with Brill 21E and also fitted vestibules to three cars, 114, 115 and 120 in the Oldham numbering.

Withdrawn

1932/33 119

July 1934 117

June 1935 113, 114, 115, 116, 118, 120

121-132. These fully enclosed cars were ordered from English Electric in October 1925; the first three were delivered by March 1926 and the remainder shortly afterwards. The cost was £20,885. 15*s.* 0*d.* (£490,000). They seated 64 comprising 22 in the saloon and 42 upstairs and were fitted with leather seats throughout. The lower saloons had three windows with corresponding windows on the upper deck.

Equipment: Brill 21E trucks 7'6" wheel base; cars 122, 126 and 129, and possibly others, were fitted with truck covers but these were subsequently removed because of corrosion problems.

Withdrawn

Aug. 1946 122, 125 and 128 were sold to the Gateshead Company becoming 68, 69 and 70 respectively and continued to operate there until March 1951.

Brakes

Early cars were fitted with Hewitt & Rhodes pneumatic brakes. An air compressor on the car axle pumped air into a reservoir located under the car seat, the pressure being maintained at 40 lbs per square inch. The maintenance cost was very high and Mr. Wilkinson suggested that in order to economise, the compressors should be dispensed with by adding three more reservoirs, which would be charged at the depot. Trials were carried out with four reservoirs of four feet length and one foot diameter fitted to a car. The experiments were made at a pressure of about 100 lbs per square inch with satisfactory results and economy; Wilkinson suggested that if the system were adopted generally the pressure should be 200 lbs per square inch for space and cost saving. In response to queries from the Board of Trade it was stated that the storage cylinders would be about 10 or 11 inches in diameter and 3 or 4 feet long and would be "specially made to withstand this pressure without any fear of them breaking". He pointed out that the track brake was rarely operated and used such a small quantity of air that once the reservoirs were charged there would always be a good margin of pressure for immediate use "sufficient in fact to keep a car going all day without having to be recharged". If it was thought that a greater supply was required it could be arranged for the cars to be recharged every journey whilst in service.

Late in 1904 Wilkinson designed and fitted a new type of track brake to one of the Oldham cars which received favourable comment at the Tramway Conference in Liverpool. The slipper block was forced onto the rail by means of two cylindrical adjustable springs held in compression and acting directly on the block; it could be brought into action either slowly or immediately as required. The block was raised and lowered by a small hand wheel on the car platform but for emergency stops it could be applied by depressing a foot lever to give its full power instantaneously. The driver therefore had full use of his hands to work the controller and hand brake handles since the track brake did not require any further attention once applied. Tests showed that on a single truck single deck car weighing about 7 tons travelling at 10 miles an hour on a gradient of 1 in 11 the car could be stopped by the track brake alone in 13 yards. It was capable of preventing a car running backwards on an incline if suddenly deprived of current.

After the Salem Brow accident in December 1912 Oldham purchased a mechanical track brake designed by Charles Henry Spencer, brother of the then Bradford Manager C. J. Spencer, for trial purposes. This brake had been approved for Huddersfield's use by the Board of Trade in September 1909 and it was in due course fitted to most of the Oldham single truck cars. It comprised a cast iron shoe 3'3" long which could be applied instantly by turning the hand wheel mounted concentrically with the hand brake staff on each platform, and locked in position. At the bottom of a steep gradient the brake was released by knocking the "dog" out of the ratchet, allowing the spring loaded mechanism to release the shoe which then rose clear of the tracks. Being completely independent of electrical circuits it could be applied or released with the car either stationary or in motion.

Works Cars

Snow Plough

In August 1902 it was decided to visit Bolton and Bradford to inspect snow ploughs and tower wagons. The outcome was a decision in December to order a snow sweeper from Brecknell, Munro and Rogers, Bristol; this was delivered in 1903 and cost £757. 10*s.* 0*d.* (£35,000). It was eventually given the fleet No. 3, possibly shortly after the passenger car of that number was dismantled in February 1915. Early in 1921 Oldham purchased welding plant principally for welding and grinding rail joints, and this was demonstrated on 12th May. Shortly afterwards it was mounted on works car 3 which ceased to be regarded as a snow plough. In December 1931 the vehicle was dismantled; the truck and motors were overhauled and transferred to the water car (see below).

Water Car

Oldham purchased a water tank for £50 (£2,300) in the year to March 1903 and in the following year incorporated it into a water car at a further cost of £361. 6*s.* 1*d.* (£17,000). It was eventually given the fleet number 38 possibly shortly after the passenger car with this number was involved in the accident in December 1912. The tank had a capacity of 1,600 gallons and took 15 minutes to fill. The spray was at the front and covered the road width, operated by air compressor. It travelled at 4 m.p.h. and cost £2. 10*s.* 0*d.* (£120) for 9 hours operation. As mentioned above it received the truck and motors from the welding plant transporter in December 1931; it was dismantled in September 1942.

Salt Trucks

Two were constructed by Oldham late in 1905 and withdrawn in 1937 being replaced by a two ton lorry.

Tower Wagons

There were originally two horse drawn tower wagons. A motor tower wagon was obtained in September 1911, after inspection of the vehicles in use at Manchester and Salford on 13th December 1910; Oldham preferred the Salford type.

In 1924 Oldham accepted a tender by Walker Vehicles Ltd to supply an electrically operated tower wagon. In 1930 one of the original Leyland single deck buses, No. 2, was converted to an overhead tower wagon.

General

The livery of the first four cars was basically dark blue but following cars were painted in brown; at the opening of the through service to Manchester in 1907 the livery was described as yellow and chocolate. The basic colour was altered again in March 1931 to crimson lake. The cars were fitted with cushions but these were removed in August 1908.

Cars were originally fitted with route boards, examples of which are:

Cross St., Glodwick & Star Inn
Lees Brook Market Place Hollinwood
Middleton Rd., Star Inn
Middleton Road King St. Hollinwood
Hathershaw Oldham
Waterhead Oldham Piccadilly

These were replaced by destination screens and boxes in 1911. The following list is from one of the indicators of car 112 and was probably standard for the system from about 1924 onwards.

Special Car; Football Match; Star Inn; Higginshaw; Copsterhill Road; Royton Boundary; Watersheddings; Butler Green; Heron St.; Circular Route; Werneth; Ashton; Summit for Rochdale; Hathershaw for Ashton; Royton; Depot Only; Moorside; Grains Bar; Hollinwood via Hollins; Middleton; Market Place; Mills Hill Bdg.; Waterhead Lees; Hollinwood via Werneth; Manchester; Oldham; Chadderton Road; Shaw (Wren's Nest); Mumps via Hollins.

In the early years the trams displayed a coloured light to indicate the route:

Route	Colour
Hollinwood - Waterhead	Red
Hollinwood - Lees	White
Middleton Road - Star Inn	Red
Circular	Blue
Hollinwood - Moorside	Green
Royton - Hathershaw	Yellow
Shaw - Werneth Fire Station	Blue
Shaw - Chadderton Road	Yellow
Lee Street - Mumps Bridge	Red & Green

Although it was decided in October 1916 to introduce route number indicators, these were not in fact fitted until 1920 and in July it was decided to advertise the fact. The numbers and routes were:

1. Hollinwood and Waterhead
2. Hollinwood and Lees
3. Middleton Road and Market Place
4. Circular
5. Hollinwood and Grains Bar
6. Hollinwood and Moorside
7. Summit and Hathershaw
8. Shaw and Hollinwood

9.Shaw and Chadderton Road
10.Union Street West (Lee Street) and Waterhead.
11Hollinwood and Market Place
12.Star Inn and Grains Bar
14.Star Inn and Ashton (from 2nd July 1921).
20. Oldham and Manchester.

A few years' experience led to the introduction of a larger route number in April 1924; the cars were modified over the ensuing three years. In 1927 side destination screens and boxes were also introduced.

Plate105. Maker's photograph of balcony car 96.

APPENDIX 2 - FARE COLLECTION

ORIGINALLY, fares were collected by the insertion of coins in a collecting box, but it was soon appreciated that this system was open to abuse, and in June, 1901, the Oldham accountant suggested "a more satisfactory fare collection system". Accordingly, tickets printed by Williamson, Ashton were introduced. These tickets were specific to the individual routes indicating the places between which the passenger could travel for the fare paid. In December 1901 it was decided to introduce metal tokens for use by Corporation staff, as appropriate, for tram travel. In December 1902, some tickets were withdrawn following complaints about an "objectionable advertisement" on the reverse. The Committee "expressed its surprise on learning the nature of the advertisement". A year later it was decided to abolish stages on the circular route and to charge 1*d.* (20p) for any distance, including a complete circuit. In April 1904 stopping places at roughly 200 yard intervals were introduced. Previously there had been no fixed stops.

There was a complaint in June 1905 from the Trade Union that Williamson was not paying fair wages, but nevertheless, Oldham continued to purchase its tickets from this printer. Following representations by the Trades Council, weekly tickets at favourable rates were introduced on 13th November. A 10*d.* (£2) ticket covered a 2*d.* journey each way daily, Monday to Saturday (a five-and-a-half day working week in those days!); for those wishing to return home at lunchtime, a 1s-6d ticket covered 22 journeys. The corresponding charges for 3*d.* tickets were 1*s.* 3*d.* and 2*s.* 3*d.* respectively, whereas for 4*d.* journeys the charge was double that for the 2*d.* issues. The tickets were not transferable and for use the week of issue only. On the outward journey the tickets were available on any car leaving the terminus up to 8.15 a.m. on Monday and up to 7.45 a.m. on Tuesday to Saturday. The return journey could be made anytime up to 6.30 p.m. departure from the terminus, with availability on Saturday restricted to a 12.30 p.m deadline.

Also from the same date ordinary work people's fares were charged on cars leaving the terminus up to 7.00 a.m., with return by cars leaving the terminus between 5.15 and 6.00 p.m. Mondays to Thursday, 5.00 - 6.00 p.m. on Friday and 11.45 a.m. - 12.30 p.m. on Saturday.

At this time the maximum fare was 3*d.* (59p), and the minimum 1*d.*, with intermediate fares at ½*d.* intervals. The longest route was Hollinwood - Moorside, 4 miles 1,521 yards. There was a single fare of 1*d.* on the circular route, the complete circuit of which was 2 miles 757 yards. Other journeys available for 1*d.* ranged from 1,493 yards for the Middleton Road-Star Inn route to 2,558 yards from the Royton boundary to Werneth Fire station on the Shaw-Werneth Fire Station route. The success of the weekly tickets was such that availability was extended in the evening from 6.00 p.m. to 8.00 p.m. departures. Basic through fares were 1*d.* Mumps Bridge to Lee Street and Middleton Road to Starr Inn, and 3*d.* for the remainder namely Waterhead to Hollinwood, Werneth Fire Station to Shaw, Hathershaw to Summit, Lees to Hollinwood, Hollinwood to Moorside and Shaw to Chadderton Road.

It was decided in May 1906 that children between the ages of three and twelve could travel at half fare. In July 1908 it was considered necessary to place notices in the trams asking passengers to destroy their tickets after use. In May 1909 Oldham declined Manchester's suggestion to cut the fare between the two towns. Later in the year, in September, it was decided to abolish the weekday time limit for return journeys using workmen's contract tickets but to extend the deadline to 1.00 p.m. on Saturdays; possibly because of wartime conditions the workpeople's weekly tickets were discontinued from August 1915.

Because of inflation it was necessary to increase tram fares from 29th April 1918. Under this revision all fares were in pence, 1½d. and 2½d. being merged in the 2*d.* and 3*d.* stages. Workmen's 2*d.* return tickets increased to 3*d.* (27p), and the 3*d.* to 4*d.*; all ½*d.* fares for children were discontinued. The through fare Hollinwood-Waterhead became 4*d.*, with seven penny stages and the same applied to Hollinwood-Lees and Summit-Hathershaw. Shaw-Chadderton became 4*d.* with eight penny stages whilst Hollinwood-Grains Bar was 5*d.* with nine penny stages. Exceptionally, the circular route fare was 1½*d.* Further increases took place on 19th May 1919 to cope with post-war inflation.

In May 1921, concern was expressed by a councillor that tickets were being issued by conductors without the use of a punch and that these were cancelled by the conductor making a tear in the ticket. It was felt that this practice could lead to dishonesty and the loss of revenue to the department. Mr.

Chamberlain said that there was a shortage of ticket punches because some were being repaired and deliveries of new punches were awaited. Generally speaking there were enough for the normal traffic but not for the holiday services. He commented that a conductor could not make any extra money if he used the tickets for which he was responsible. "The punches were really an extra check and not always used. Their absolute check was the number of tickets sold. If there was any question about that then they fell back upon the punch check". It was pointed out to Mr. Chamberlain that there was nothing to prevent an employee from collecting the tickets left in the car and reissuing them. He agreed that could always be done but "it was infinitely more difficult to punch a ticket twice in the same place". Mr. Chamberlain pointed out that he was rather keen about making money. "If they were short of punches there could, of course, be a general order that no car should go out without a punch. He did not give any such order, however, because he wanted the brass". The Committee decided to press for delivery of the punches on order.

Another fares revision came into effect on 3rd July 1922 when a 1*d.* (9p) minimum was again available. The distance which could be travelled varied from 611 yards from Middleton Road terminus to St. Andrew's Church to 1,404 yards between Count Hill Road and Moorside. Through fares now ranged from 1½*d.* on the Middleton Road and circular routes to 5½*d.* (52p) on the Hollinwood–Grains Bar and Hollinwood–Shaw routes. Any one child under five years old not occupying a seat was carried free of charge but generally the fare was half the adult fare with a minimum 1*d.*, rounding up if necessary, up to age 12.

The following month, special tickets were introduced for circular tours in Wakes weeks which covered the Ashton and SHMD systems in addition to Oldham. In February 1923 it was decided to fit boxes for used tickets on the platforms, but not all trams were equipped until about September. Manchester had introduced used ticket boxes in 1910, and both systems used identical wording, namely "please deposit used tickets in this box".

With an easing in post-war inflation it was possible to reduce fares from 3rd September 1923 generally by extending the fare stages to roughly pre-war levels. Thus a 1*d.* fare now ranged from a low of 1,267 yards for the Villa Road–Star Inn stage of the Hathershaw–Summit route to a maximum of 1 mile 350 yards between Higginshaw boundary and Shawside on the Chadderton Road–Shaw route. The maximum through fare was 5½*d.* (55p) for Hollinwood–Grains Bar (5 miles 1,570 yards), whereas Hollinwood–Shaw (5 miles 461 yards) was 5*d.* On the acquisition of the Chadderton section of the Middleton Electric Traction Company in 1925, the through fare Market Place–Mills Hill Bridge was 2½*d.* (25p) for a distance of 2 miles 770 yards.

A dispute in the coal mining industry in 1926 cost the department an additional £6,000 (£150,000) for electricity as a result of which it was necessary to increase fares temporarily on 24th December. The 1*d.*, 1½*d.*, 2*d.* and 2½*d.* ordinary fares and the workmen's daily return fares were increased by ½*d.* The normal fares were resumed on 8th July 1927. The colliery dispute led to a general strike as a result of which the whole of the Oldham transport operation, in common with others, was closed from 4th May to 12th May 1926 inclusive.

On 18th June 1928 the intermediate ½*d.* fares were abolished by an increase of ½*d.* on these fares, but the 1*d.*, 2*d.*, 3*d.*, 4*d.* and 5*d.* fares were unchanged. No through fares changed except that the complete circle on the circular route now cost 2*d.* (21p) instead of 1½*d.*

Tokens were also in use as a means whereby employers could pay for workers to travel by tram. In October 1929, Manchester suggested to Oldham that these celluloid items issued by the various operators in the Manchester area should be of a uniform colour. It was proposed that 1d tokens should be red, 1½*d.* blue, and 2*d.* yellow, but Oldham disagreed because it would have to replace its tokens at a cost of about £140 (£3,500). It was also thought that there would be disadvantages in financial checks. Also on 6th November it was decided to increase the workmen's return fares from 2*d.* to 2½*d.*, 3*d.* to 4*d.* and 4*d.* to 5*d.* (52p); however, the previous charges were reinstated on 12th May 1930.

On 14th July, a minimum 1½*d.* (17p) fare was introduced for a stage of approximately 1½ miles. Other fares remained unchanged apart from the circular route where a flat charge of 1½*d.* was introduced compared with 1*d.* stages and 2*d.* for a complete circuit. Special cheap return tickets at about 25% below the ordinary fares were also introduced, available between 10.00 a.m. and 5.00 p.m. for use on the return journey at any time on the day of issue. They were withdrawn on 31st January 1931 because they had failed to attract additional passengers.

A general increase in fares and stages came into effect on 25th March 1931 although penny fares were re-introduced for a stage of approximately three-quarters of a mile. Intermediate half-penny fares were also reintroduced. The effect of these increases on through journeys was that the 4*d.* through fare for Hollinwood–Waterhead increased to 5*d.* (58p), that for Hathershaw–Summit from 5*d.* to 5½*d.* whereas Hollinwood–Shaw, Wren's Nest, increased from 5*d.* to 6½*d.* (75p). Shaw– Chadderton Road also rose by ½*d.* to 5½*d.* but the fare to Mills Hill Bridge remained unchanged at 3*d.* Hollinwood–Market Place rose from 2*d.* to 2½*d.* and on the circular route the flat fare of 1½*d.* gave way to fares of 1*d.* and 1½*d.* with 2*d.* for a complete circuit. The general tightening was further evident when on 11th May free riding facilities which had been available since 1907 to members of the police force in uniform and on duty were withdrawn.

Substantial reductions in fares were introduced on 18th August 1935. As an illustration the through fare Hollinwood–Waterhead came down from 5*d.* to 3*d.* (36p) with the fare from each terminus to Market Place being reduced from 3*d.* to 2*d.*; Hollinwood–Shaw was cut from 6½*d.* to 3½*d.* whilst Hathershaw–Summit was reduced from 5½*d.* to 3½*d.* These fares still applied at the outbreak of war in 1939, but the last mentioned had gone over to buses as previously related. The fares on the Hollinwood–Waterhead route were still unchanged in early 1942.

Plate 106. Former Oldham tram 128 as number 70 of the Gateshead and District Tramways Company is seen here in Newcastle-on-Tyne on its way to Wrekenton on 29th August 1948 and thus two years after being withdrawn from service in Oldham. Further from the camera is Gateshead 35, formerly Oldham 24 on its way to Haymarket.

Photo, W. A. Camwell.

OLDHAM CORPORATION PASSENGER TRANSPORT DEPARTMENT

SHAW (WREN'S NEST) and HOLLINWOOD VIA WERNETH.

On and from Sunday, December 3rd, 1939, Motor Omnibuses will operate the above service in substitution of Tramcars.

The following revised time-table will be introduced :

MONDAY TO FRIDAY.

Shaw to Hollinwood.				Hollinwood to Shaw.			
5-20 a.m.				6-0 a.m.			
6-0 a.m. and every	15	minutes until	8-30 a.m.	6-30 a.m. and every	15	minutes until	8-15 a.m.
8-50 a.m. ,,	20	,,	5-30 p.m.	8-40 a.m. ,,	20	,,	5-0 p.m.
5-45 p.m. ,,	15	,,	6-30 p.m.	5-15 p.m. ,,	15	,,	6-15 p.m.
6-50 p.m. ,,	20	,,	10-10 p.m.	6-40 p.m. ,,	20	,,	10-20 p.m.

SATURDAY.

5-20 a.m.				6-0 a.m.			
6-0 a.m. and every	15	minutes until	8-30 a.m.	6-30 a.m. and every	15	minutes until	8-15 a.m.
8-50 a.m. ,,	20	,,	11-30 a.m.	8-40 a.m. ,,	20	,,	11-0 a.m.
11-45 a.m. ,,	15	,,	12-30 p.m.	11-15 a.m. ,,	15	,,	12-15 p.m.
12-50 p.m. ,,	20	,,	10-10 p.m.	12-40 p.m. ,,	20	,,	10-20 p.m.

SUNDAY.

1-50 p.m. and every 20 minutes until 10-10 p.m.   2-0 p.m. and every 20 minutes until 10-20 p.m.

The existing Workpeople's Services will also be operated by Motor Omnibuses.

WALLSHAW DEPOT,
OLDHAM, Nov. 24th, 1939.

J. F. RICHARDS
GENERAL MANAGER AND ENGINEER

APPENDIX 3 - GENERAL MANAGERS

Richard Henry Wilkinson - February 1902 - September 1904.

Born in Liverpool, Mr. Wilkinson was apprenticed in mechanical engineering with the British and African Steam Navigation Company Limited. He was awarded a Board of Trade Certificate for marine engineering in October 1898 and the following month was appointed assistant to the general manager of Liverpool Corporation Tramways. In December 1900 he became Tramway Superintendent at Oldham being made General Manager in February 1902. In September 1904 he was appointed General Manager at Huddersfield where he remained until October 1918 when he was appointed General Manager of Bradford City Tramways. He retired through ill health in September 1930 and died in Bournemouth on 13th December 1943.

Lewis Slattery - October 1904 - January 1911.

Mr. Slattery was 36 years old on appointment. In 1884, he became a clerk with the Bury, Rochdale & Oldham Steam Tramways Company. In 1889 he took a position in Hartlepool, followed by a spell in Blackburn, being appointed General Manager of the Blackpool, St. Annes & Lytham Tramways Company Limited in 1896. Following his period at Oldham he became Chief Traffic Superintendent of the London County Council Tramways. He was subsequently appointed General Manager of West Ham Corporation Tramways, a position he still held at the time of his death on 28th August, 1932.

Joseph W. Dugdale - February 1911 - March 1916

Mr. Dugdale, aged 41 on appointment, was Traffic Superintendent of the Sheffield Corporation Tramways and in September 1903 was appointed Manager of the City of Oxford and District Tramways Company Limited. His tenure was brief because in July 1905 he was appointed Manager of Ashton Corporation Tramways, a position he held until he became Manager at Oldham. He had unsuccessfully applied for the position when his predecessor was appointed in 1904. He resigned in March 1916.

Percy Priestly - April 1916 - April 1918

Mr. Priestly, aged 41 on appointment, served his engineering apprenticeship with Sir William Allan Limited in Sunderland. After leaving Sunderland he had five years marine experience, gaining a first class Board of Trade Certificate. In 1901 he was appointed Assistant Engineer of the Halifax Corporation Electricity undertaking and ten months later became the Borough Electrical Engineer. In August 1907 he was appointed Manager of the Mexborough and Swinton Tramways Company, which he converted from the Dolter surface contact system to overhead current collection. He remained with this company until his appointment as Manager at Oldham. He left Oldham to become Deputy Manager of the Liverpool Corporation Tramways, a position which had originally been offered to Mr. J. S. D. Moffet, Manager of the Belfast Tramways, who had declined it on receiving an increase in salary at Belfast. Mr. Priestly was appointed General Manager in succession to Mr. C. W. Mallins in February 1920, and died in office on 13th March 1933.

William Chamberlain - May 1918 - April 1925

Mr. Chamberlain was born in Lancaster in 1878. His career began in the Lancaster Corporation Electricity Department followed by two years as Chief Engineer at the Wallasey Electricity Works. This was followed by a spell as Electrical Engineer to the Merseyside Harbour Board.

In 1902 he was appointed Mains Superintendent at the Oldham Corporation Electricity Works becoming one of the joint borough electrical engineers in 1904, from which position he was appointed Manager of the tramways. He had been an unsuccessful candidate for the position in April 1916. He left Oldham on being appointed General Manager of the Leeds Corporation Tramways, a position he held until 1928 when he moved to Belfast to occupy a similar post. He resigned this position on 1st December 1930, to the new appointment of North West Region Traffic Commissioner, one of twelve appointments established under the new Road Traffic Act.

Clement Jackson - July 1925 - November 1929

Mr. Jackson, who was born in 1893, was a native of Huddersfield and was indentured to Sheffield Corporation Tramways where he passed through the workshops and power station becoming Motor Works Superintendent. He joined the forces in 1915 and was subsequently commissioned to the North

Midland Territorials. He served in France and Belgium from 1916 onwards and was awarded the military cross in 1917, achieving the rank of captain. He returned to Sheffield at the end of the war and was appointed General Manager of the Keighley Corporation Tramways in June 1922.

On leaving Oldham he became General Manager of Plymouth Corporation Transport, a position which he had until retirement. He died in 1955.

John Frederick Richards – December 1929 – October 1943

A native of London Mr. Richards served his time with the Metropolitan Electric Tramways Company, passing through all departments. He then became Chief Draughtsman and Technical Assistant to the rolling stock superintendent of the West Ham tramways. During the first World War he served in the technical section on aeroplane design at Hendon but after two years was transferred by the Ministry of Transport to the West Ham system, where the rolling stock was in a particularly bad state through unavoidable overcarrying of munition workers.

He then became Technical Assistant to the General Manager of the Belfast Corporation Tramways moving in November 1921 to the position of Works Superintendent at Oldham. He died in office in Oldham on 4th October 1943, aged 55.

Cyril Percy Paige – March 1944 – September, 1961

Mr. Paige was born at Sevenoaks, Kent, and served with the Royal Flying Corps for over four years in the first World War, and for a period afterwards was Engineer to the Eastbourne Aviation Company. After acting as Manager of Ashby Motor Services Limited, Tunbridge Wells, he was General Manager and Engineer to Bangor Blue Motors Limited in 1922, becoming, in 1925, the Local Manager (Eastern area) for the Yorkshire (West Riding) Electric Tramways Company Limited, and the West Riding Automobile Company Limited, Wakefield. He was appointed Manager of Bury Corporation Tramways in 1933; on appointment at Oldham he was 47. He retired on 30th September 1961, and was succeeded by his deputy, Mr. H. Taylor who had been appointed in December 1959, being then Technical Superintendent at Liverpool City Transport.

Plate 107. Maker's photograph of all-enclosed car 24 at the Grains Bar terminus.

APPENDIX 4 - OPERATING STATISTICS

Year to March	Mileage Run	Passengers	Traffic Receipts £	Total Receipts £	Net Working Expenses Excluding Power £	Power £	Gross Profit £	Finance Costs Inc. Tax £	Surplus £	Receipts Per Car Mile d.	Trams	Year End Route Length Miles	Yards
a1901	14628	216238	901	1054			220			17.29	b4	b3	572
c1902	212425	2124259		8851						10.00	b31	b11	594
1903	1275148	10779371	47662	48220	23199	15673	9348	17063	(7715)	9.08	b80	b17	352
1904	1420432	12968880	59322	60403	29667	13608	17127	24594	(7827)	10.20	80	17	352
1905	1505929	13466481	65651	66841	29147	15686	22007	26183	(4176)	10.65	80	17	352
1906	1753546	16668026	84321	85912	29540	19307	37065	29780	7285	11.75	80	23	122
1907	1818444	18647731	92981	94949	33425	21581	39942	30615	9327	12.53	80	23	122
1908	1978150	20082367	99937	101481	37323	24303	39855	30844	d9011	12.31	80	23	122
1909	2055450	19929973	99551	100651	42108	27100	31443	32636	(1193)	11.75	80	23	122
1910	1867762	18455837	92373	94577	44124	23753	26700	31779	(5079)	12.15	80	23	122
1911	1893777	19125202	95975	97843	46359	23218	28266	29950	(1684)	12.40	80	23	440
1912	1942147	20073483	101280	102099	49094	22090	30915	33329	(2414)	12.62	92	23	827
1913	2049916	21435727	108003	110577	51967	21470	37140	32591	4549	12.95	92	23	1109
1914	2077104	22773108	114481	116170	57739	20564	37866	32660	5206	13.42	92	23	1109
1915	2045840	22171712	111679	113814	65342	19742	28730	33948	(5218)	13.35	109	23	1146
1916	1983607	23477066	118339	121129	62149	19441	39539	35426	4113	14.66	108	24	0
1917	2010604	24670848	124958	127284	64872	20571	41841	36330	5511	15.19	97	24	0
1918	2121092	28703371	148582	151412	84784	22153	44474	37496	6978	17.13	93	24	22
1919	2093946	31229035	181585	184030	101255	23082	59693	39548	20145	21.09	93	24	22
1920	2124755	31816891	234680	237409	143035	25613	68760	42187	26573	26.82	93	24	22
1921	2202868	32071037	245617	250742	174592	27644	48506	43422	5064	27.32	106	24	22
1922	2460699	32402875	248869	253883	170317	30186	53379	36656	16723	24.76	105	24	22
1923	2608696	32140449	238261	241652	148494	31078	62079	43536	18543	22.23	104	24	22
1924	2620805	33410901	217596	219892	146579	30406	42907	33519	9388	20.14	102	24	22
1925	2654196	36364299	213783	215615	14888S	29967	36763	32928	3835	19.50	108	23	1645
1926	2725331	38532238	226728	230652	162332	29496	38824	32706	6118	20.31	116	25	1110
1927	2684867	34491193	217602	227547	160730	34928	31889	31524	365	20.34	122	25	1110
1928	2821437	34916106	220884	225720	160712	28237	36770	32753	4017	19.20	119	25	1110
1929	2712132	35091134	205597	207061	143024	25022	39015	33541	5474	18.32	118	22	99
1930	2518387	32938207	192012	192701	131621	23938	37142	32382	4760	18.36	117	22	99
1931	2421678	28323004	176134	176776	120013	22667	34096	31020	3076	17.52	111	22	99
1932	2433734	28219545	170702	171681	115981	21347	34353	30111	4242	16.93	111	22	99
1933	2373519	26639825	156819	157767	111145	20104	26518	17932	8586	15.95	110	22	99
1934	2373273	26383608	153284	153883	109939	19656	24288	16252	8036	15.56	110	21	1598
1935	2386419	26794112	154273	154932	109227	17108	28597	19863	8734	15.58	109	21	1554
1936	1832816	20256364	110082	110647	92485	10341	7821	12699	(4878)	14.49	69	14	842
1937	1506836	16061733	84217	84762	71448	7871	5443	6991	(1548)	13.50	68	14	842
1938	1282399	13792140	73056	73473	62547	6991	3935	10739	(6804)	13.75	44	7	1622
1939	866347	9440723	50196	50787	53046	5284	(7543)	6978	(14521)	14.07	44	7	1622
1940	753209	9079536	48701	48956	43149	4503	1304	5909	(4605)	15.60	27	4	96
1941	547383	8505993	46734	46582	40803	3756	2023	4630	(2607)	20.42	27	4	96
1942	512799	9191727	49391	49599	41259	4004	4336	3797	539	23.21	27	4	96
1943	509302	9542228	51706	51914	42116	4002	5796	4869	927	24.46	27	4	96
1944	510363	9664092	52493	52702	46107	4042	2553	5814	(3261)	24.78	27	4	96
1945	408366	8507550	48660	48868	46268	3874	(1274)	4179	(5453)	28.72	27	4	96
1946	441659	8508309	50111	50318	49180	4287	(3149)	3701	(6850)	27.34	27	4	96
e1947	152743	3073602	19715	19891	21768	1441	(3318)	921	(4239)	31.25	27	4	96

a) 15/12/1900 to 30/6/1901
b) June
c) 15/12/1900 to 3/1902
d) of which £3,000 to rate relief
e) to 3/8/46

( ) = loss